THE COMPLETE LANCASHIRE COOKBOOK

by
Catherine Rothwell

edited by
Sylvia Hayes

PRINTWISE PUBLICATIONS LIMITED

Published 1993
© Printwise Publications Ltd
47 Bradshaw Road, Tottington, Bury,
Lancs, BL8 3PW.

Warehouse and Orders
Unit 9c, Bradley Fold Trading Estate,
Radcliffe Moor Road,
BOLTON BL2 9RT.
Tel: 0204 370753
Fax: 0204 370751

The recipes have originally been published in four other books.
LANCASHIRE RECIPES, ISBN 0 86157 018 09
MORE LANCASHIRE RECIPES, Published 1984
RIBBLE VALLEY RECIPES, Published November 1986
MERSEYSIDE RECIPES, ISBN 0 86157 263 7
© Catherine Rothwell
plus additional recipes and hints

Recipes edited by
SYLVIA HAYES

Concept and book designed by

Cliff Hayes

Printed & Bound by
Manchester Free Press, Longford Trading Estate, Thomas Street, Stretford,
Manchester M32 0JT. Tel: 061 864 4540

ABOUT THE AUTHOR

Catherine was born in the Prestwich area of Manchester and has resided on the Fylde Coast of Lancashire for the past thirty years. During her career she has been Deputy Borough Librarian of Fleetwood and after re-organisation, in charge of all Local History and Reference for the Lancashire District of Wyre.

Catherine's articles frequently appear in such quality magazines as 'Lancashire Life', 'The Lady' & 'Lake Scene'.

Her success in writing has led to appearances on B.B.C. and Granada Television, and Catherine has been interviewed on B.B.C. Radio Lancashire, Radio Piccadilly, Coventry and Warwick, Isle of Man Radio and Red Rose Radio. She enjoys lecturing to the W.E.A. and to local Associations and Groups.

Catherine with Husband Eddie and two of their Grandchildren, Eleanor and Patrick.

Dedicated to grandchildren Eleanor, James and Patrick.

ACKNOWLEDGEMENTS

The obviously old recipes are mainly "family", all are of Lancashire origin and for them I am grateful to my late mother, Mrs E. Houghton; my late great-aunt, Mrs F. Fielden; Miss Marion Stott, Honorary Treasurer of the Lancashire Federation of Women's Institutes; and Mrs Jenny Gibson of Cleveleys.

I thank my husband, without whose help I could not have coped: appreciative, willing food taster and faithful companion in many weathers. We both remember with fondness the spirit of hospitality and kindness encountered almost everywhere, plus all the thank yous and acknowledgements in the original books.

Take time to treat yourself to a culinary trip to the past. It is well worth the effort.

INTRODUCTION

Since collecting material for *Lancashire Recipes Old and New* and its three companions my opportunities to sample traditional fare of other counties have brought my total of cookery books to twelve. Throughout, my aim has been to publicise tried and tested favourites based on fresh local ingredients.

Meeting such a great number of people in my search for family recipes has also revealed extensive information about cooking methods and the most suitable utensils, often with an interesting history. I tracked down a potter making pipkins, sometimes known by their old-fashioned name of 'piggins', dating back to the days of Elizabeth I. because of their pot-bellied shape these are ideal for individual casseroles, retaining heat and giving delicious flavour.

Lancashire is justly famed for its fare and I found that many Lancashire recipes had found their way to other counties, for reasons such as Lancashire girls cooking for their Cornish or Devon husbands.

Although the book harks back to the days of old-fashioned cooking in fire ovens, these dishes can be made in modern ovens. You can have the best of both worlds by using blenders and food mixers to take the hard work out of chopping and creaming. The most satisfying food is that bought fresh and presented within a short time. What is fundamental to all recipes is that they embody wholesome ingredients prepared cleanly and briskly with the minimum of fuss. However many times you dish up a family favourite like braised silverside of beef on a bed of parsnips (just add 1 bay leaf and a cup of water) it never becomes boring. It's the flavour that wins hearts and which caused Lord Byron to say, "Since Eve ate apples, much depends on dinner."

The pleasure of a coal fire, the taste of toast made on a fork over glowing embers, the aroma of chestnuts roasting, home made toffee, kippers cooking on a griddle, apple fritters, will all bring back memories which it is our duty to pass on.

Catherine Rothwell
February 1993

CONTENTS

                                                                       Page No

Soups 7
Fish 12
Main Courses 21
Snacks & Savouries 39
Chutneys, Pickles & Accompaniments 49
Invalid Foods 57
Puddings & Pies 60
Cakes, Scones,
Breads & Biscuits 76
Jams & Sauces 100
Cold Sweets & Toffee 104
Drinks 113
Old Remedies 119

COOL OVEN	225-250 F 110-120 C
SLOW OVEN	275-300 F 140-150 C
MODERATE OVEN	375 F 190 C
HOT OVEN	425-450 F 220-230C
VERY HOT OVEN	475-500 F 240-260 C

Soups

CHINESE CHOWDER

13 ozs Chinese leaves
2 large onions
2 large tomatoes

2 tablespoons peanut butter
½ pint vegetable stock

Shred the leaves very fine and put in a pan with the stock. Cook for 5 minutes at the boil. Meanwhile chop finely the tomatoes and onions, having previously removed the tomato skins by dropping them in boiling water and peeling. Add to the pan, stirring in the peanut butter. Cook over gentle heat for 10 minutes. Season to taste and serve hot.

COCKIE LEEKIE

5 large leeks
A prepared cock or hen
(1½lbs of stewing beef, cut up, can be used instead)

Thoroughly wash the leeks and scald in boiling water. Remove roots and part of the tops. Cut into pieces about half an inch long. Put the hen flesh or beef meat into the pot with half of the leeks. Simmer gently with a tablespoonful of pearl barley for half an hour. Add the remaining leeks and boil for three hours. Skim and season to taste with pepper and salt. Serve with fresh, crusty bread.

CUCUMBER SOUP

1 good-sized cucumber chopped and peeled with seed removed

1 pint chicken stock
1 small onion chopped

Boil together until tender then place in a liquidiser. Thicken with a little cornflour mixed with a little milk. Re-heat and finally serve with a swirl of cream on top.

COURGETTE SOUP

1 finely chopped medium onion
1½ pints chicken stock
salt and pepper
1 oz butter
1 lb courgettes

Melt butter in saucepan and add onion. Wash and trim courgettes, cut into thick slices and add to onion. Stir in hot stock. Bring to boil, cover and simmer for ½ hour. Cool slightly and liquidise. Season to taste. Can be served hot or cold. Serves 4.

QUICK CARROT AND LENTIL SOUP

This is almost a meal in itself

2 cups lentils soaked overnight
8 ozs lean bacon
(trim off all fat)
½ teaspoon salt
a sprinkle of herbes de Provence
1 chopped, cleaned leek
3 large carrots
scraped and chopped
freshly ground black pepper
¾ pint vegetable stock

Drain lentils. Place ingredients in pressure cooker and add stock. Pressure cook for 15 minutes as lentils need to be very well cooked. Release pressure and place in liquidiser for about a minute. Reheat and serve with crisp rolls. It may be necessary to thin the soup with a little hot water, especially if some is stored in the fridge until next day.

HALEWOOD HERB AND VEGETABLE SOUP

½ pint water
1 chicken stock cube
1 good-sized potato
2 medium carrots
1 medium onion
2 handfuls red lentils
1 dessertspoon tomato purée
¼ teaspoon thyme
¼ teaspoon sage
¼ teaspoon celery salt
1 pinch marjoram or oregano
small clove of garlic
1 cup brown beer or
1 glass red wine

Using a large saucepan, dissolve stock cube in water. Chop all vegetables and add other ingredients to pan. Bring to boil then stirring occasionally, simmer until vegetables are soft. Add water to compensate for that boiled away as the soup thickens. Before serving, top up with milk to produce a smoother finish.

KIDNEY SOUP

1 ox kidney
1 marrow bone
1 carrot
Some sprigs of parsley
Pepper and salt to taste

Cut the kidney into small squares, having removed the fat. Soak for one hour in boiling water. Wash thoroughly and place in stewpan with sufficient water to cover. After having brought quickly a-boil allow to stew slowly for $1\frac{1}{2}$ hours.

Preparing the stock: Place the marrow bone with carrot and sprigs of parsley into another saucepan and pour over these 2 quarts of water. This must boil for $1\frac{1}{2}$ hours at the end of which, the bone, parsley and carrot must be lifted out. Now add to this prepared stock the contents of the first pan, and having seasoned, boil all together for 1 hour. The soup must be skimmed thoroughly before serving.

LENTIL SOUP

$\frac{3}{4}$lb red lentils
1 large onion
A little celery
1 marrow bone

1 carrot
1 turnip
Salt and pepper to taste

Clean the lentils by washing in a colander. Finely chop the onion, celery, carrot and turnip. Place all in a pot with 1 pint of good stock and 1 ounce of butter. Boil for three hours. The soup can be strained or not as desired.

LEEK SOUP

1 large potato
3-4 medium size leeks

$\frac{1}{2}$ small onion
sprinkle of herbs

Wash well, peel potato, split leeks, rinsing layers under cold running water, cutting off bottoms and ragged tops, but retain sound green parts. Chop all up and cook with one pint of chicken or vegetable stock until tender. Season. Place in liquidiser for about one minute. Reheat and serve with toasted wholemeal bread and watercress.

PEASANT SOUP

2oz butter
2lb stewing steak cut into cubes
2 large chopped onions
1 bay leaf
1 crushed garlic clove
1 sprig of thyme
4 chopped sprays of parsley

½ teaspoon black pepper
4 pints beef stock
4 tablespoon flour
Pepper to taste
2 large peeled chopped potatoes
1 teaspoon of dried dill
2oz grated cheese

Melt the butter in a heavy saucepan. Add the beef and onions for 5 minutes until browned. Mix in the flour; stir in the stock. Bring to boil. Add the rest of the ingredients apart from the dill and cheese which should be scattered on top of portions when served, and simmer for 2 hours.

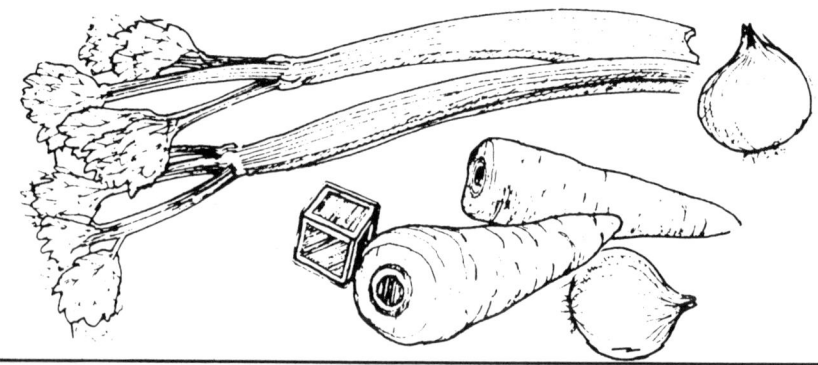

SPRING SOUP

As the year moves on to March and April a good spring soup is recommended ... "for Spring converts the frozen state of Winter at a better rate ..."

8oz potatoes
8oz leeks
1oz butter
8oz young nettles

2½ pints of chicken stock
1½oz watercress
¾ pint of cream
Salt and black pepper

Peel and slice potatoes. Wash well and chop the nettles and leeks. Melt the butter in a large saucepan, stirring in potatoes and leeks. Cook gently for 15 minutes. Add the stock and the chopped nettles, bringing all to the boil, then simmer. The watercress can be added whilst the soup is cooking towards the end. Use a blender then return the soup to a clean pan. Stir in the cream and reheat it carefully stirring all the time. This soup is very good with wholemeal bread.

WATERLOO PEA SOUP

12oz dried peas or split peas
3 pints stock from boiled
   ham or bacon shank
2 thinly sliced onions
pinch of dried mustard
seasoning to taste

Soak peas overnight in boiling water. Next day throw away water. Put all ingredients into pan, bring to boil, cover and simmer very gently for 2-3 hours, adding extra liquid if needed. Cooking time can be reduced if soup is pressure-cooked.

WINTER BROTH

1 lb washed, diced vegetables
   (carrots, turnips, leeks)
4 ozs shredded cabbage
1 pint vegetable stock
1 bay leaf
1 teaspoon mango chutney
1½ pints boiling water
1 oz rolled oats

Simmer the chopped vegetables in the stock with the bay leaf for 20 minutes. Add the cabbage, chutney and oats; simmer for a further 15 minutes. Remove the bay leaf. Serve very hot with buttered toast "soldiers".

WATERCRESS SOUP

Wash 3 bunches of watercress, discarding coarse stalks. Fry the watercress gently in 1oz butter but save a few leaves for decoration. Add 1½ pints vegetable stock to the pan with a little salt and simmer for 15 minutes. Liquidise and put back into pan. Blend 1oz cornflour with a little milk taken from ½ pint. Pour the rest of the milk into the pan and bring to the boil, then add the cornflour mixture and simmer for 4 minutes. Serve with a swirl of single cream and watercress leaves floating on top of the soup portions.

Fish

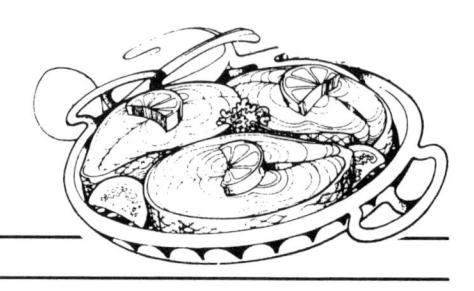

WIRRAL FISH PIE

7oz tin tuna
1oz margarine
1 tablespoon chopped parsley
½ pint milk
salt and pepper

1 large or 2 small hard-boiled eggs
1lb boiled potatoes
4oz Cheddar cheese grated
1oz plain flour

Flake the tuna and put into a greased oven-proof dish 1½ to 2 pint size. Make the parsley sauce with the margarine, flour, milk and parsley and season as required. Slice the hard-boiled egg and arrange over the tuna. Cover with the parsley sauce. Mash the potatoes and mix in the grated cheese. Use this to cover the fish, eggs and sauce. Cook for 20 minutes at 200°C. Serves 3-4.

FISH CAKES

½ lb cooked white fish
2 teaspoons lemon juice
1 tablespoon chopped parsley

½ lb creamed, seasoned potatoes
2 tablespoons beaten egg to bind

Remove any skin and bone from fish and flake it up. Add potatoes to fish plus the chopped parsley, lemon juice and beaten egg with any desired additional seasoning. Smooth mixture well with a wooden spoon and turn onto a floured board. Shape into 6 rounded cakes about 1 inch thick. Brush with beaten egg and fry in deep cooking oil until golden brown, or in shallow fat, turning, if preferred. Serve on a hot dish garnished with parsley and lemon slices.

FISH CASSEROLE

1 lb cod or haddock
9 ozs skinned tomatoes
9 ozs cheddar cheese
¼ pint thin cream

freshly ground pepper
pinch of sea salt
chopped parsley
juice of 1 lemon

Sprinkle the lemon juice over the fish and season. Grease a dish with butter. Put in half the cod, then half the tomatoes, adding more seasoning. Cover with sliced cheese. Top this with the remaining cod and tomatoes. Pour the cream over all and sprinkle the parsley on top. Bake in a hot oven. Serve with a side salad containing plenty of fresh, sliced tomatoes and lemon juice on the greens.

TRAWLER PIE

2 lbs mashed potatoes
1½ lbs haddock or cod
4 ozs mushrooms
4 ozs peas
2 ozs butter
1 pint of milk

Wash the fish well. Wash, slice and cook the mushrooms in a skillet with a little butter. Poach the fish, adding a little vinegar to the poaching liquid, then flake it well, removing any bones and fish skin. Place the mashed potato round the edge of an oven-proof dish, leaving room for the flaked fish in the centre. Dribble a little milk over all and on top place the sliced, cooked mushrooms and peas. Cover all this with a plain sauce and bake for 30 minutes in a moderate oven. Freshly snipped chives are very tasty on this dish as a garnish.

KILLINGTON FRIED TROUT

Clean, scale and remove fins, tail etc. with sharp, kitchen scissors. Do not split open. Dip in oatmeal, salt and pepper. Heat some butter in a heavy frying pan; lay in the trout and brown well. Serve thickly strewn with minced, fresh parsley and lemon quarters.

RIVER TROUT WITH LEMON

Juice of one lemon
4 trout cleaned
flour for coating the fish
3 ozs butter
4 ozs breadcrumbs
lemon slices and sprigs of parsley

Half the lemon juice should be poured over the trout and left for 15 minutes. Season and coat each fish with flour. Fry the trout for just 15 minutes in a little cooking oil, turning to brown both sides. Toss the breadcrumbs into the butter and brown these prior to sprinkling them over the trout. Garnish with the lemon slices and more parsley with more lemon juice available for those who want it. Have all ready, for this dish needs to be served piping hot.

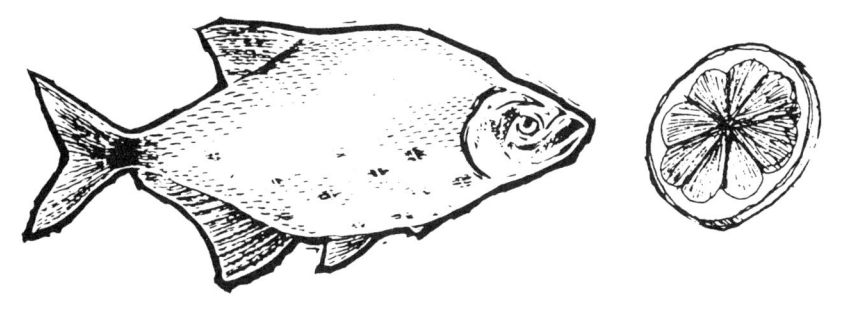

SALAMGUNDI

8 ozs smoked salmon (pre-sliced)   2 ozs prawns
2 ozs melted butter   2 ozs cream
chopped parsley   black pepper
lemon juice   salt and pepper to taste

Take 4 ozs smoked salmon; lay them flat on a piece of greased greaseproof paper to form a rectangle 6 ins x 4 ins. Place rest of smoked salmon and all other ingredients into a blender until a smooth paste forms. Season to taste. Place mixture into centre of rectangle. Roll tightly and refrigerate for 12 hours till firm. Slice with a hot knife and serve two slices per person, garnished with cucumber, water cress and fresh parsley. Serve with melba toast or brown bread and butter.

SEA-FOOD FANTASY

2 ozs butter   4 ozs prawns
4 ozs diced halibut   4 ozs salmon tail
½ oz mild curry powder   2 ozs finely chopped onion
½ oz diced red pepper   ½ diced fresh pineapple
1 teaspoon mango chutney   ¼ pint double cream
sea salt   ground black pepper

In a medium-sized saucepan melt the 2 ozs of butter. Add the finely chopped onions and curry powder. Cook for one minute without browning. Add the red pepper and pineapple and cook for a further 2 minutes, then add the halibut and salmon; cook for an additional 2 minutes. Pour in the double cream, mango chutney and prawns and simmer for 5 minutes.

Season to taste and serve with rice. It can be garnished with whole cooked prawns (with shells on) and parsley.

LUNE SALMON

2 good-sized Tail Ends of Salmon
2 tablespoons of Snipped Chives

Put the fish into a pan and cover with water. Bring to the boil and simmer for five minutes only. Take out of the pan; save the liquor. Remove the skin and bones from the fish. Cut it into fair-sized pieces. Put it back into the pan with two cups of the fish stock and the chives. Cover and simmer very slowly for twenty minutes. Serve with cucumber and sprigs of parsley. Don't forget to eat the parsley. It is said to be good for kidney complaints.

SALMON MOULD

1 medium-sized tin of salmon or cooked fresh salmon
1 tablespoon milk
1 breakfast cup of fine brown breadcrumbs
pinch of salt and pepper

Pound this well together and put in a greased pudding basin. Cover well and steam for 2 hours. Serve with green salad and mashed, creamed potatoes.

STUFFED MACKEREL

4 mackerel gutted, cleaned and fresh
4oz chopped mushrooms
salt and pepper
2oz butter
1 small chopped onion
2 teaspoons chopped parsley
slices of lemon
2oz cooked rice

Mix together, rice, onion, parsley, seasoning and half the mushrooms. Bind with the melted butter. Stuff the mackerel with this mixture. Fold together and wrap tightly in foil. Bake the 4 separate foil parcels at 200°C for a good $\frac{1}{2}$ hour. The remaining mushrooms should be sautéd in butter, the parcels unwrapped carefully, saving any juice from them to cover the fish. Garnish with lemon slices and sautéd mushrooms.

HERRINGS

Herrings, once so plentiful and cheap they were a nourishing standby for poor people, have now become both scarce and expensive. The tasty, humble kipper, derived from the herring, is approaching the smoked salmon class. Good Manx kippers soaked overnight in lemon juice need no further cooking. After draining off the liquid, remove the bones; mash the kippers with a little butter. Spread on brown bread; it tastes good. Cooking on a gridiron over a glowing, open fire or charcoal brings out the best in any kipper. Serve with scrambled egg.

Fresh herrings can be baked or grilled after rolling in oatmeal, like trout. A typical workman's meal sixty years ago was prepared as follows:
Clean and fillet six herrings. Roll them up and pack tightly into an earthenware, fireproof dish on top of three bay leaves. Sprinkle thickly with finely chopped onions. Cover with a white vinegar and water solution (half a cup of each). Cover with a lid and bake in a moderate oven for 40 minutes. If left overnight in the liquid, these can make a delicious and nourishing breakfast.

SOUSED HERRINGS OR MACKEREL

4 small herrings or mackerel
¼ pint vinegar
2 thin slices onions
¼ pint water
1 bay leaf

Scale and trim fish, remove heads, split open and remove backbone. Wash and dry fish. Sprinkle with salt and peppercorns from a mill. Roll up from head to tail, packing the fish side by side in a heat-proof dish (porcelain is ideal). Pour over sufficient vinegar and water to cover. Add bay leaf and onions. Cover dish and bake half way down the oven at 190°C. for 40 minutes. Remove from liquor, drain and cool. A bed of green salad garnished with tomato makes a good accompaniment.

KEDGEREE

1 lb cooked smoked haddock
6 ozs Patna rice
3 ozs butter

Garnish with one chopped, hard-boiled egg and one tablespoon finely chopped parsley mixed together.

Boil rice for 10-15 minutes, washing it first and adding 2 teaspoons of lemon juice to the water. It should be drained well and put to dry off at bottom of warm oven. Poach the haddock, removing any skin or bone. Flake the cooked fish. Melt butter in a saucepan, add rice, seasoning and heat gently for 15 minutes. Pile on heated dishes and garnish.

SKEM KEDGEREE

Quick, easy and savoury

2oz butter
2oz cooked long-grain brown rice
sprinkle of sea salt and black pepper
½lb beef sausages
2 chopped hard-boiled eggs
1 tablespoon chopped fresh parsley
¼ teaspoon mild Madras curry powder

Melt 1oz butter in a pan and gently fry the sausages split down the middles. Cook until golden brown. Add the cooked rice, more butter, curry powder and chopped eggs. Stir the whole mixture constantly over low heat and cook thoroughly. You may need to add a little warm water carefully, to keep it smooth and workable. Finally add seasoning and the sprinkling of chopped parsley. Serve very hot. This is good with any of the chutney recipes.

BROMBOROUGH FISH PIE

1lb fresh haddock or cod
4oz prawns
2oz butter or margarine
1 pkt onion sauce mix
3oz grated Cheddar cheese
paprika

salt and pepper
6oz mushrooms
2 tablespoons chopped parsley
1lb potatoes cooked
2 tablespoons cream

Poach fish with seasoning in about $\frac{1}{4}$ pint water for 10 minutes. Place drained, flaked fish in a greased pie dish and add prawns and chopped mushrooms. Make up the onion sauce with 1oz margarine, using the fish liquor and stir in parsley. Pour the sauce over the fish. Mash the potatoes with other ounce of margarine, grated cheese and cream. Season if necessary. Spread potato over the fish and sprinkle a little paprika on top. Bake for 20-25 minutes or until top is golden at 200°C. Serves 4-6.

EEL PIE

3 lbs. Eel skinned and cut up
4 tablespoons of Corn Oil or Olive Oil
6 ozs. of Chopped Onion
About 20 Button Mushrooms

Salt and Pepper
Butter and Flour
Lemon to garnish

Toss the eel in flour seasoned with salt and pepper. Brown the eel pieces in a pan containing hot oil. Take out the eel and lightly saute the onion. Return the eel slices to the pan; add the mushrooms, seasoning and a pint of water. Simmer for thirty minutes. The eel sauce can be thickened by gradually adding small lumps of butter, kneaded with flour, stirring all the time to keep it smooth. Serve hot, garnished with slices of lemon.

Eel pie is cooked as above, put in a pie dish, covered with a pastry top and baked at 400°F for thirty minutes.

A member of a Fleetwood family that dates back to when the town began in 1836 has described eel-spearing in the many ponds which used to line the areas of Broadway, Hambleton, Over-Wyre. The eels, caught with a long-poled, metal tri-pronged implement, were stuffed in a bag and towards evening taken home for stewing or making into pie.

BAKED HADDOCK

Scale and clean the fish without cutting it open too much. Put in a delicate forcemeat - one egg and bread crumbs with pepper, salt and chopped parsley. Sew up the slit and brush the fish all over with egg, sprinkle with bread crumbs. Put some good dripping in the tin and baste the haddock frequently whilst baking. Garnish with parsley and cut lemon and serve with plain, melted butter.

STEWED PLAICE

Clean, trim and scale a fresh plaice. Put into a stewpan with a little stock suitable for white meat (can be prepared from the fish trimmings). When the stock boils, put in the plaice. Lay pieces of butter on top. Well dust it with flour, pepper and salt to taste. Cook slowly for half an hour and serve with its own sauce.

POTTED SHRIMPS

Morecambe Bay shrimps have been prized as delicacies for three hundred years.

1 lb. Fresh Shrimps *¼ teaspoon Cayenne Pepper*
5 ozs. Clarified Butter *Sea Salt*

Put the shrimps in boiling water and cook for two minutes. Cool and remove from shells. Melt 3 ozs. of the clarified butter with cayenne and salt. Put the shrimps in an oven-proof dish and pour the seasoned butter over them. Bake for thirty minutes (350°F.). Remove from oven; drain and cool. Pack the shrimps into small jars; pour over the strained butter in which they were cooked. Leave to set, then cover with the remaining clarified butter – about ¼ in. thick.

FLEETWOOD BATTERED SHRIMPS

An old Fleetwood recipe tosses freshly-picked shrimps into batter and fries them immediately; they are eaten straight from the pan.

SHRIMP SOUFFLE OMELETTE

4 eggs
1 teaspoon flour
½oz butter

8 tablespoons cream
pinch of salt
shrimps

Mix yolks of eggs smoothly with the flour, salt and cream. Whisk the whites very stiffly and add lightly to the mixture. Heat butter and pour the eggs into an omelette pan without stirring. Cook for about 4 minutes over low heat and finish under grill. Fold in half and turn onto a hot dish. Garnish with the following:

Melt ½oz butter and stir in 1 teaspoon flour. Add 4 fl oz milk. Stir till it boils and boil for 3 minutes. Wash shrimps and heat them for 5 minutes in the sauce. Add 1 tablespoon cream, dash of pepper and a squeeze of lemon. Garnish round the omelettes in small heaps. Anything tasty, such as mushrooms, chicken or sweetbreads could be warmed in the sauce and used as garnish.

LYTHAM SHRIMPS CLIFTON

12 ozs peeled shrimps
1 clove of garlic
1 teaspoon brandy
sea salt
sippits (to top)

2 ozs butter
¼ pint double cream
cracked black pepper
2 ozs parsley

In a small saucepan, melt the 2 ozs of butter. Finely chop the garlic, add to the butter and stir. Then add the shrimps to the butter and garlic, stirring constantly for about 30 seconds. Add the brandy, flambé and pour in the ¼ pint of cream. Simmer for 2 minutes. Season to taste with cracked black pepper and sea salt.

Divide into 4 equal portions and garnish with sippits and chopped or sprig parsley.

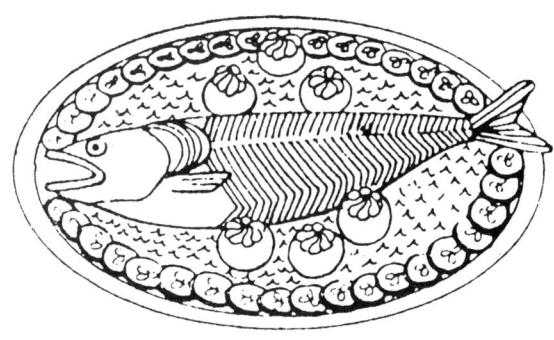

SCALLOPED LOBSTER

If you are fortunate enough to obtain a fresh lobster, treat it as directed in 1883.

1 Fresh Lobster *Pepper, Salt, Butter*
Bread Crumbs *2 Pints of Stock*

"Crack up the lobster and simmer in the stock for about half an hour. Add some Lancashire Relish, chopped shallott and chopped parsley. Cool. Extract the lobster meat; arrange in scallop shells; sprinkle with bread crumbs and dot with butter. Place in oven till lightly browned". Nowadays, placed under the grill and served immediately would perhaps be more convenient.

LANCASHIRE LOBSTER

A new way with lobster, for a special occasion, is to make it into a souffle.

1 Lobster *1 Tablespoon Chives*
1 Pint water *½ oz. Gelatine*
1 Onion *¼ Pint Double Cream*
1½ ozs. Flour *3 Egg Whites*
1½ ozs. Butter

Remove flesh from the lobster and place in a bowl. Crush shell and simmer in water for one hour with the onion. Strain off and keep. Melt butter; stir in flour; add stock; put in the snipped chives and flaked lobster. Dissolve the gelatine in a little hot water and add to the gently simmering lobster mixture, but do not boil. Cool well. Stir in the cream and fold in the stiffly beaten egg whites, making sure that no grease of any kind is on the bowl or the beater and that not a speck of yolk has wandered in. Chill and serve in a souffle dish.

Main courses

SHOULDER OF LAMB

. . . with Wild Thyme or Rosemary . . .

This old method of wrapping lamb in a parcel with herbs is much as the Greeks have done for centuries.

One half shoulder of lamb
2 cloves of garlic
Freshly ground black pepper
Sprigs of wild thyme or rosemary

Insert snippings of the garlic into slits made in the lamb. Oil a sheet of muslin (greaseproof paper is better), seasoning the paper well. Lay the sprigs of thyme or rosemary on the paper and put the lamb on them, covering the lamb with the rest of the herbs. Wrap up the parcel and put it into a roasting tin in a hot oven for two hours, by which time the lamb will be subtly flavoured throughout.

Flowers, fruit and herbs used in cooking and drink-making were gathered when the dew had dried off them and before the sun became too hot. The fruit should be just ripe. This cough remedy must be very old as it came from the 1860 fragment previously referred to.

PORK WITH APRICOTS

2 lbs pork tenderloin
1 oz flour
10 dried or canned apricots
vegetable stock

2 ozs butter
1 glass white wine
1 teaspoon arrowroot
4 ozs blanched apricots

If dried, the apricots will need soaking overnight. If canned, drain and rinse. Cut the pork into wide strips of about 4 inches across. On each fillet place almonds and apricots with a fillet on top. Dust with flour. Add the stock and put in a roasting tin covered with foil. Cook for 2 hours at 180°C. The remaining apricots can be cooked in the wine. Add the liquid from the apricots to the meat juices, thicken with arrowroot and pour over the pork. More almonds can be used to garnish. Melted butter enriches the sauce but is optional.

COUNTRY LAMB HOT POT

2 lbs lamb
8 ozs onions
1½ lbs potatoes
1 pint vegetable stock
1 lb carrots

Trim any fat off the washed lamb and cut into pieces. Peel and slice onions; chop carrots; slice potatoes. Place the seasoned lamb in the casserole with alternate layers of vegetables and meat. Finish with a layer of potatoes and season well between the layers. Sprinkle the top with half a teaspoonful of herbes de provence. Pour in stock and cover with casserole lid. Cook for 2 hours at 180°C. Serve with buttered braised celery.

ROAST PILLING LAMB

Before roasting, wash the joint of lamb and rub gently with coarse salt; pour over the juice of half a lemon and scatter with dried Rosemary leaves. The time required for cooking varies with the size of the joint. Pilling lamb is best served with fresh-made mint sauce, the recipe for which comes from nearby Preesall.

4 ozs. Mint Leaves; 6 ozs. Sugar; ½ pint Malt Vinegar

Chop the mint finely. Boil the vinegar; pour it on the mint and sugar. When the sugar has dissolved by stirring it with a wooden spoon, pour into wide-mouthed, clean jars almost to the brim. Allow to cool, then seal.

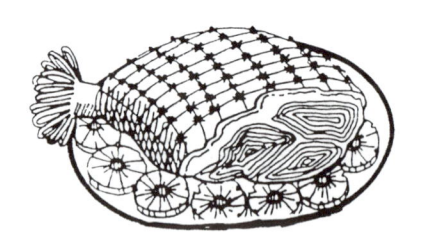

BEEF & HAM ROLL

1 lb. Lean Shoulder Steak
½ lb. Ham
1 beaten Egg
1 cup Breadcrumbs
Seasoning
1 teaspoon Chopped Parsley

Mince the ham and steak and mix with the breadcrumbs, seasoning and chopped parsley. Bind with the beaten egg. Steam in a greased pudding basin for 3½ hours. This goes very well with buttered swedes or carrots well mashed and chopped, boiled onions or spinach.

SHEEPS HEAD BROTH

Place a sheep's head and trotters into a large bowl or can of salt and water and soak all night. In the morning scrape well, rinse in running water, place in a large pan and boil with sufficient water to cover, adding ¾ cup of barley, ¾ cup of peas, 1 small turnip cut into squares, 2 diced carrots, 2 blanched leeks, pepper and salt to taste. Boil for 3 or 4 hours then strain off the broth into a tureen and serve immediately.

Hog's head, sheep's head or boar's head could be the basis of a dish going back to the Vikings. In the sixteenth century and before there were no vegetables apart from peas and beans; bread ("maslin") was a mixture of coarse grain, rye and oats; sweetening consisted of honey from bees. The paddock at the "toft" or homestead had a patch of oats, barley or wheat. Herbs were used to mask the taste of meat "going off" and there was no fresh meat in winter except from pigeons kept for that purpose in a special pigeon house and these were for the Lord of the Manor and his family.

Mother hated preparing sheep's head but it had to be done because father roared for it like a Viking. It tasted good and I'm sure it was nourishing but I have never been bold enough to cook one myself or to make black puddings. Aunt Kate was not afraid to tackle ox heads and ox feet.

Bannocks, cooked on a girdle or griddle to go with either, come from "bruni" which is pure Norse.

LANCASHIRE HOT POT

Some cooks now use stewing beef cut up into cubes to make hot pot, it being simpler to handle, but real hot pot is made using middle-neck lamb chops. It was always served with pickled red cabbage at our house.

8 Middle-neck Lamb Chops
4 Lamb Kidneys, sliced
½ lb. Sliced Onions
Salt and Pepper
½ pint Stock
2 lb. Sliced Potatoes

Trim excess fat from chops. Put a layer of potatoes in a deep, oven-proof dish; lay some of the chops on top; cover with a layer of kidneys and onion. Make similar layers, seasoning each with salt and pepper. Finish with a layer of potatoes. Pour over the stock and brush the potatoes with melted butter. Cover with a lid and cook in the oven for two hours at 350°F. Remove the lid; increase the temperature and cook for another thirty minutes to brown the potatoes. My mother used to add trimmed slices of bacon on top to crisp, at this stage. An updated version of hot pot is to add successive layers of tomatoes plus a bouquet garni then the final touch of bacon slices.

TRIPE AND ONIONS

When King Cotton reigned in Lancashire, every village and city had its tripe shop. Tripe and onions was reckoned a nourishing, cheap dish for the workers and tripe-dressers probably outnumbered fish and chip shop proprietors. My uncle, who became Treasurer in a London borough, made an annual pilgrimage back to his native Lancashire for the express purpose of dining off tripe and onions. Here's how mother made it after we children returned laden from the shop in Whittaker Lane, Heaton Park.

2 lbs. Dressed Tripe
¾ lb. Sliced Onions
1½ pints Milk

2 ozs. Butter
1 oz. Flour
Nutmeg, Seasoning

Cut the tripe into narrow strips about 2 inches long. Simmer the tripe and onions in the milk for about one hour until tender. Melt the butter in a pan; stir in the flour and cook for a few minutes. Gradually add the milk from the tripe to make a thick sauce. Bring to the boil and season with nutmeg and salt. Add the tripe and onions; heat through and serve with mashed potatoes.

LIVER AND BACON

1 lb. Liver
½ lb. Bacon
1 oz. Flour
2 Onions

Salt and Pepper
1 teaspoon Chopped Parsley
2 ozs. Dripping or Butter
½ pint cold water

Slice the liver ½ inch thick; wash thoroughly; dry and leave in a cloth for ½ hour before cooking. Fry the sliced bacon; dip the liver in half of the flour and all the seasoning. Fry along with slices of onions and remove to a hot dish. Add the rest of the flour to the pan; pour in the water, stirring well with chutney to make an appetising colour and use this as gravy, serving the liver on top of the bacon.

BEEF CURRY

This curry was being made long before there were any Indian Restaurants in the Valley and it can take its place proudly. The secret lies in the long, slow cooking, 8 hours if possible, done in the oven in a well-sealed casserole. Allow at least 2 inches clearance in the container you choose, as there is a gentle bubble-up. There is a good helping here for three in the quantities given.

¾ pint marmite stock
2 ozs Madras curry powder
3 ozs plain flour
½ lb braising steak
 cut into cubes

1 large baking apple
 (Bramley for choice)
1 medium onion
large handful sultanas
juice of a whole large lemon

Chop the onion and apple. Put into a steel pan containing 3 ozs butter. Gently cook for 10 minutes. Stir in the curry powder and flour, slowly pouring in the stock. Allow another 10 minutes, stirring the while. Have ready in the casserole the cubed meat and lemon juice. Spoon the contents of the pan upon this mixture and scatter the handful of sultanas upon it. Stir. Cover the casserole and place in centre of oven.

Long-grain brown rice is an excellent accompaniment. Wash the quantity required, cover with boiling water and cook for 15 minutes. Drain. Place around the curry portions. Serve with mango chutney, slices of tomato and banana.

Buy good quality beef. It is a fallacy to think good curry can be made from poor meat, which in any case it would be unwise to cook in a slow oven. Never use cooked, left-over meat.

TO MAKE CURRY

2 large onions
1lb of meat or small chicken or rabbit
2 large tablespoonfuls of curry powder

1 lemon
A breakfast cup of milk
4 cloves and a bit of cinnamon

Fry the onions, sliced in butter, till brown. Remove them and lay on a plate. Into the butter mix the curry powder, first moistened with four teaspoonfuls of water. Let it fry, stirring very carefully until it begins to look dry and brown, then add the diced meat and fry it in the curry powder for a very short time. Add the milk and allow it to simmer until it thickens. Add the fried onions, powdered spices, lemon juice and salt. Simmer long and very slowly.

". . . if you like to add vegitables, the spices must be left out . . ." These are Mary Anne's own instructions - and spelling!

I found this curry too basic and tried again, adding a handful of sultanas, one grated cooking apple and a tablespoonful of coconut. Surprisingly, the use of a Slo Cooker did not give the best result, which I think is obtained by slow cooking in the oven, in an earthenware casserole.

TO BOIL RICE FOR CURRY

Have a clean pan half filled with boiling water seasoned with salt. Put in quantity of rice required. Boil quickly for 15 minutes, stirring occasionally with a clean, wooden spoon. Strain through a colander and run cold water on it. Let it drip, then put the colander into an empty stew pan and stand near the fire (or oven heat), turning it lightly till perfectly free, fluffy and dry. Serve round the curry.

LENTIL CURRY

6oz lentils
1 large onion
1 clove garlic
1 dessertspoon curry powder
squeeze of lemon juice

1 bay leaf
1 small apple
$1\frac{1}{2}$ tablespoons oil
1 small can baked beans
3ins chopped cucumber (optional)

Wash and soak lentils then cook gently with bay leaf until tender. Peel and chop onion and apple, crush garlic and fry together in oil with curry powder for 15 minutes. Add lentils and baked beans, lemon juice to taste and cucumber if using. Serve with rice or creamed potatoes. This quantity is sufficient for two. Quick to make and any left over can be used cold with green salad.

LIVERPOOL LOBSCOUSE

$\frac{1}{2}$lb breast of lamb
3lbs potatoes
1 pint water or vegetable stock
1 small black pudding chopped up
good sprinkle of mixed herbs

$\frac{1}{2}$lb stewing steak
$\frac{1}{2}$lb carrots
$\frac{1}{2}$lb parsnips
1 large onion

sea salt and a dash of pepper

Peel potatoes. Wash and trim meat. Cut up. Peel vegetables. Cut up. Place all together in a stew pot or pan. Bring to boil and simmer slowly for 2 hours, adding more liquid if required but do not "drown" the lobscouse. A recipe resulting from S.O.S. Scouse!

KIRKBY KASSEROLE

1 pint stock or water
2 medium-sized carrots
2 large English onions
(Spanish are too mild)
cup of soaked washed lentils
oregano or basil to taste
almost 1lb lean beef mince or
 tripe or pork shoulder

1 white turnip
1 parsnip
1 leek
1 leaf red cabbage
crushed clove of garlic
no salt

Dice the vegetables after washing and peeling them. Put all in a large pan together and bring to boil. Lower heat and simmer for about 2 hours. If beef is used, dumplings can be added to the "casserole" about $\frac{1}{2}$ hour before ready, otherwise a sprinkle of parmesan cheese is good. A masculine, no nonsense recipe.

CORNED BEEF SCOUSE

1lb potatoes
1 medium onion
$\frac{1}{2}$lb carrots
1 beef stock cube

1 pint water or stock
$\frac{1}{4}$ teaspoon sage
$\frac{1}{2}$ small can of corned beef
pepper

In a large saucepan, dissolve stock cube in water or stock. Slice potatoes and carrots and add to pan together with chopped onion, sage and pepper. Meanwhile slice and cube corned beef and add to pan 15 minutes before serving. Add water to top up when necessary, remembering that scouse should have taken up most of the liquid when cooked.

BEEF ROLL

$\frac{1}{2}$lb minced lean beef
pinch mixed herbs
salt and pepper

4oz bacon rashers
2oz breadcrumbs
1 egg

Put meat in bowl, add chopped bacon and mix together. Add mixed herbs, salt and pepper and breadcrumbs. Beat the egg and bind all together. Mould into a roll shape, put on greaseproof paper. Wrap it up then roll it in a cloth and tie up with string. Drop in pan of boiling water and boil slowly for $1\frac{1}{2}$ hours. When cold, take out of cloth and paper. Cut into slices. Useful as a buffet dish garnished with salad.

Created a Life Peer in 1983, Lord Wilson of Rievaulx was M.P. for Huyton 1950-83. He likes Cornish pasties, but this Merseyside recipe could also become a favourite.

LIVERPOOL HOT POT

1lb best shin beef cut up
2 leeks
6 small peeled potatoes
¾ pint water
4 slices lean bacon

½ onion
1 heart of celery
1 large tomato
seasoning
herbes de Provence

Use a deep casserole. Wash and chop finely the ½ onion, celery, leeks (including their sound green tops), 2 potatoes and the tomato. Wash the meat and place layers of vegetables and meat with 2 sprinkles of herbs and seasoning into the large casserole. Finish off with a thick layer of thinly sliced potatoes on top. Place lid on casserole and cook in a slow oven for 3 hours. Half an hour before needed, place the slices of lean bacon on top. Swish gently the whole casserole so that gravy flows onto the top layer of potatoes. Keep the lid off so that the bacon cooks crisp and the potato topping browns.

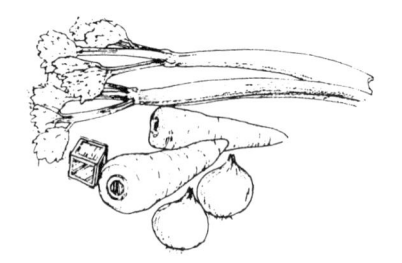

NOT LIVER & ONIONS

"This recipe is a great favourite of ours. It is very quick, very cheap, and, we think, delicious." (Bishop David and Grace Sheppard, Liverpool).

Take up to ¾lb of pig's liver (price 45 pence on October 2nd 1985). Slice each piece as thinly as possible on a board with a very sharp knife. Slice away from your fingers. Season quite heavily with black pepper and salt both sides. Take a heavy bottomed frying pan and heat through just under a table spoonful of olive oil. (Olive oil goes at least twice as far as ordinary oil in our experience). Fry quickly on both sides the seasoned pieces of liver. This may take up to five minutes depending on how hot the oil remains. For the best flavour do not overcook the liver which will cause it to go hard and leathery. Leaving the liver in the pan, add about a sherry glass full of medium sherry and fry gently until the juice is reduced a little. Turn off the gas/electricity. This meat is now ready to be eaten and tastes good with brown rice that is already prepared and waiting and hot with a prepared salad, or with any other green vegetable that is also prepared and hot. Your table needs to be laid and your plates warm as this is a very quick and delicious way of eating something that we used to dread in our schooldays.

ST. HELEN'S STEW

2lb best braising steak
1 pint beef stock
pepper and salt
1 bay leaf
1lb onions
3lb potatoes
sprinkle of herbs

Wash the meat, remove any fat and cut into short strips, tossing these in flour. Place a layer on the bottom of a large enamelled iron casserole. Follow this layer with chopped onion, sliced potatoes and some seasoning and herbs, then another layer of the floured strips of meat. Continue thus, finishing off with a layer of sliced potatoes which completely covers the meat and onions. Gently pour in the pint of stock and place in the oven with a lid on for 3 hours at 160°C. As the name suggests, it can be stewed, but better flavour results from slow oven cooking. Originated in a large household, the three pounds of potatoes were then five.

DINNER PARTY CASSEROLE

1¼ lbs chuck steak
1 oz dripping
¼ pint beef stock
½ cinnamon stick
6½ ozs cranberry sauce
¼ oz butter
1 oz flour
½ teaspoon basil
3 cloves
1 tablespoon lemon juice
parsley

Mix flour with basil, salt, pepper and coat steak cubes. Fry and brown. Put in casserole, add stock, cloves and cinnamon. Bring to boil then simmer for 1½ hours. Stir in cranberry sauce and lemon juice. Cook for 30 minutes. Blend butter with flour which remains and thicken stew. Serve with green salad and jacket potatoes.

ONIONS AND KIDNEY

8 lamb kidneys
2 large onions chopped
8 ozs small white onions
   peeled
½ pint white wine
1 tablespoon water
1 tablespoon flour
1 tablespoon mango chutney
¼ teaspoon tarragon vinegar
salt to taste

Trim and skin the kidneys, wiping them clean with a vinegar cloth. Brown the chopped onions (sprinkled with sugar) in a large nut of butter. Remove onions. Add kidneys sprinkled with flour. Stir. Add wine, water, onions chutney, browned onions, salt and pepper. Cover and simmer for 30 minutes. Serve with water cress.

SAVOURY BALLS & STEW

In a basin place half a pound of flour, 4 ozs. of shredded suet, a little minced parsley and chopped onion, salt and pepper. Mix together with a little cold water, sufficient to make a stiff dough; divide into balls; roll each lightly in flour and drop into a stew. Cook for one hour. A tasty stew can be made as follows:

½ lb. Beef cut into small squares
1 large Spanish Onion
1 Carrot
1 Turnip or small Swede

Celery Stick
pinch of Salt
Mixed Herbs
1 dessertspoonful of Pearl Barley

Simmer the meat for 1½ hours with the barley and herbs before adding the chopped vegetables and seasoning.

GRANNY BROWN'S BRAISED OX TONGUE

Wash and dry one salted ox-tongue, after soaking in water overnight. Prepare a mirepoix of vegetables (2 carrots, 2 small turnips, 2 onions, stick of celery, salt, 2 cloves, bouquet garni, 1 oz. of dripping or butter).

Heat the dripping or butter and add the vegatables, washed and cut into small pieces. Fry gently. Add the bouquet garni and place all in an earthenware dish. Put the tongue on it and pour over 2 pints of brown stock which has been brought to the boil. Cover with greaseproof paper. Put the lid on the earthenware dish and place in a hot oven. After about ten minutes reduce the heat and cook very slowly for about five hours until the tongue is tender. Remove from dish; cut away gristle; pull out any bones or skin. If the tongue is adequately cooked, the skin peels away very easily. Put the tongue into a round tin or casserole; cover with one pint of the stock to which has been added ¼ oz. of gelatine. Put a piece of greaseproof paper over and a weight upon it. After allowing to stand thus for 24 hours, it can be turned out and served sliced with dressed salad.

VEGETABLE CASSEROLE

A good, family, meatless dish

As much as we adults may scorn them, baked beans out of a tin are good body builders. This recipe serves to appease and please young appetites. Flaunt the tin with the internationally known label before you start; it is a good lead up. Supermarket red wine for dad is good to wash it all down.

2 onions
8 ozs carrots
1 large potato
½ pint vegetable stock
4 ozs baked beans
½ pint milk

2 crushed cloves of garlic
5 sticks crisp, white celery
1 oz butter
1 tablespoon tomato puree or a large chopped fresh tomato
2 tablespoons flour

Wash, peel and dice the vegetables. Gently saute in the butter for ten minutes. Add the beans, stock and half of the milk. Blend the flour with the rest of the milk and add to the casserole. Bake in a slow oven for 2 hours in which jacket potatoes can be cooking as the ideal accompaniment.

STEAK AND KIDNEY PIE

Two pounds of best beef steak are recommended in Grandma's recipe but you can "make do" with braising or stewing steak. Beat it with a hammer; cut thinly into squares and place in a pie dish with seasoning. Add a breakfast cup of cold water. Core and dice the kidney. Put all in the pie dish and cook slowly for three hours, placing a shortcrust pastry top on the dish in the last hour of cooking. Grandma used to roll the pieces of steak in finely-minced suet before putting them into the dish and I presume this helped in making the rich, brown, natural gravy. She also put the pastry lid on much earlier, covering with buttery paper if it browned before the meat was cooked. This method worked in the fire oven, but in a modern electric or gas oven the pastry would blacken and burn.

CHICKEN CASSEROLE

1 oz butter
2 ozs seasoned flour
4 chicken joints
2 ozs mushrooms

2 teaspoons chives and parsley mixed
½ pint pure vegetable stock
1 large onion, chopped

Put the washed chicken joints into a casserole and add the onions fried in butter. Make a roux sauce as follows:
   The flour should be placed in the butter in the frying pan, the stock added and all the herbs. Stir well and pour over the chicken and onions. Cover the casserole and cook for an hour at 150°C. Garnish with the cooked mushrooms.

ROAST FYLDE CHICKEN

If obtainable, a fresh-killed, free-range bird, ready-dressed. Wash well under a cold-water tap at full force. Stuff with sage and onion or chestnut stuffing. Squeeze lemon juice over the bird and cover well with buttered, greaseproof paper. Place in a hot oven; keep well basted. The length of time for cooking varies with the size of the bird, but a good roaster is not likely to need more than two hours. Allow the last fifteen minutes with the paper removed to ensure even, gold browning of the skin. Serve with apple sauce and scrubbed potatoes cooked in their jackets or peeled and browned alongside the bird. Small sprouts touched with early frost are the best vegetable accompaniment to Fylde chicken. If a Spring chicken, serve with real, garden, pod peas and new potatoes.

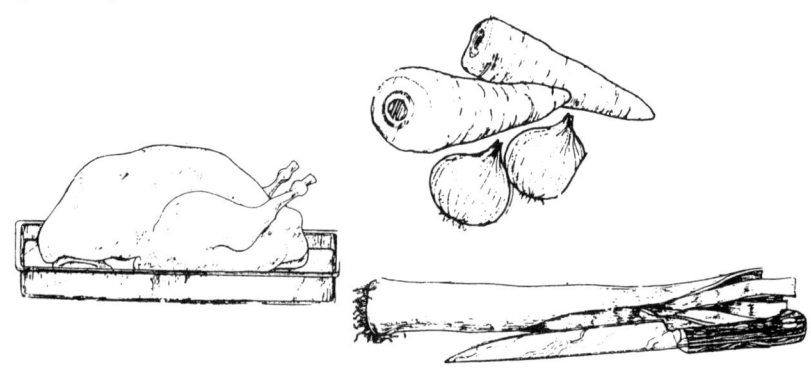

CHICKEN CHOWDER

This recipe came from an American pen friend whose grandparents emigrated from Burnley to Maryland ninety years ago. We think the origin was Burnley chicken, not Maryland. In summer when they go to the ocean they substitute clams.

½ pint chicken stock
8 ozs cooked, chopped chicken
  (chunky chicken from a tin will do)
a can or frozen pack of sweetcorn
1 tablespoon flour
8 ozs diced potatoes
2 bay leaves
½ pint milk
1 chopped onion
freshly ground peppercorns
chopped mint or parsley

Sauté onion and potatoes in a pan. Add stock, bay leaf and chicken, stirring for twelve minutes. Add milk and sweetcorn, blending the flour with some of the milk and stirring constantly till thickening takes place. Gently cook on for a further ten minutes to avoid any uncooked flour taste. If necessary, thin down with a little milk trickled carefully and slowly into the pan. The chopped parsley or mint is scattered onto the servings.

CHICKEN AND RICE PUDDING

3oz brown long-grain rice
2 tablespoons chopped parsley
seasoning to taste
8oz chopped cooked chicken
4 eggs
¼ pint thin cream

Hard boil 2 eggs, shell and chop. Cook the rice and drain it well, having previously washed and soaked it for 1 hour. Mix the chopped chicken and egg. Whisk the other 2 eggs and work this into the other ingredients: egg, chicken, parsley, rice, seasoning, cream. Pack into a well greased pudding basin and steam gently for 1 hour.

STUFFED HAM (THE STUFFING)

4 chopped apples
2 chopped onions
1 tablespoonful chopped sage
1 cup chopped parsley
2 big handfuls of bread crumbs
Salt and pepper

Bind the above together with 6 well-beaten eggs. Ham on the bone is best, the stuffing being placed into the hole left when the bone is removed. Tied tightly in a clean cloth, it was then boiled for 3 hours and allowed to go cold before the cloth was removed. In those days it was placed on a marble slab in the larder. Ham and stuffing sliced taste delicious with a salad or without.

HONEY ROAST

1 joint of best gammon
cloves
8 ozs English honey

Soak the joint to get rid of the brine, frequently changing the water. This is most important for flavour. Wrap the joint in foil and cook at 180°C. in a tin, allowing 20 minutes to the pound according to weight of gammon. A quarter of an hour before cooking time is up, remove ham from foil, score the rind with a sharp knife and push in a few cloves. Spread the honey all over the ham and return to the oven, basting with the juices plus a little water which have collected in the roasting tin. Within the last 15 minutes the ham turns a succulent-looking brown.

   This traditional joint slices up very well when cold and is still a favourite for high tea or the "Sunday-go-to-meetings" occasion.

GLAZED GAMMON

4lb piece of middle gammon
2 level teaspoons prepared
   mustard
4oz demerara sugar
1 bay leaf
cloves

Soak the gammon in successive changes of cold water to free it of brine. Place gammon in large pan with a bay leaf. Cover with fresh cold water and bring slowly to boil. Remove any scum and simmer for 2 hours until tender. Allow 20 minutes to the lb and 20 minutes more. Mix mustard with 1oz sugar. Leave gammon to cool in liquid. Remove and drain. Rub the mustard and sugar mixture well into the ham. Dust with remaining demerara sugar. Score the gammon with a sharp knife in a diamond pattern, pushing a clove into the centre of each diamond. Cook for a further 20 minutes until golden brown in centre of oven at 180°C. Serve cold, garnishing the slices with cucumber.

PORK EN CROUTE

8 ozs puff pastry
1 small chopped onion
2 tablespoons cranberry sauce
small cup of red wine
1 pork fillet
1 orange - zested and juice removed
salt, black pepper, bay leaf

Marinade overnight pork loin in all ingredients except pastry. Roll pastry out and brush with juices. Seal pork fillet in hot fat and place in pastry. Fold over and seal. Bake in a moderate oven for 10 minutes or until pastry is golden brown. Reduce rest of juices in pan till pouring consistency is reached or thicken with arrowroot. Serve accompanied with Julienne of carrots. See recipe for Puff Pastry.

SEAFORTH SWEET & SOUR PORK

2 pork steaks
1 medium onion
2 medium cooking apples
1 small tin plum tomatoes
$\frac{1}{4}$ teaspoon sage
black pepper and salt

Grease inside of shallow oven-proof dish. Place sliced apple and tomatoes into base. Cut pork into bite-sized pieces and spread over tomatoes and apples. Sprinkle sage, pepper and salt. Cover dish with baking foil and cook one shelf above centre of oven at about 200°C until pork is tender.

SPRING CLEANING STEW

As its name suggests, the general upheaval of eighty years ago when the entire house was cleaned from floor to ceiling left little time for elaborate, lengthy cooking. Spring Cleaning Stew could be quickly prepared, left to simmer long and no doubt was gratefully ladled out in the evening and much appreciated after toil.

> *2lb lean pork cut into two-inch strips*
> *Thinly sliced large onion*
> *4oz mushrooms washed and sliced.*
> *4 celery stalks trimmed, washed and chopped*
> *3 cups of chicken stock*
> *Salt and pepper to taste*
> *2 teaspoons of flour*
> *2 teaspoons of lemon juice and the finely grated*
> *Rind of lemon*

Although the old recipe does not mention this, I think the pork strips are better browned in hot cooking oil first, for at least ten minutes, as pork needs to be thoroughly cooked. Then put all in a stew pan, stirring in the flour to thicken. Simmer slowly for at least two hours, better still longer, topping up with a little water if necessary, but with a good fitting lid, no attention suffices.

TO STEW A RABBIT

Cut up the rabbit into nice pieces. Put them into a stewpan with ¼lb of butter, six good-sized onions sliced, 3 bay leaves and a little parsley. Simmer all very gently for two hours and a half or three hours over a slow fire, stirring constantly. When the rabbit is done, remove the bay leaves, place the rabbit in the dish as you would cutlets and fill the middle with the onions. The gravy should be made from the trimmings of the rabbit and at the last put in it a tablespoonful of redcurrant jelly, thicken it with a little flour, give it a boil up and strain it into the dish. This description is of an 1860 method of preparation.

RABBIT WITH ONION SAUCE

1 rabbit
1 carrot
1 teaspoon sea salt
10 rolls of grilled bacon

3 large onions
1 bouquet garni
1 pint water

THE SAUCE

1 oz butter
¾ pint stock in which the rabbit
   was cooked

1 oz flour

Cut up vegetables. Wash rabbit well and put in sufficient boiling water to cover. Add herbs and vegetables but do not boil. It must simmer to produce tenderness. It takes about an hour.

To make the sauce, melt butter, add the flour and mix well. Put in ¾ pint of the liquid in which the rabbit was cooked and stir the sauce until it boils. Cook for four minutes.

Chop the onions well and add to sauce. Pour the sauce over the rabbit which should be kept hot and garnish all round with grilled bacon rolls.

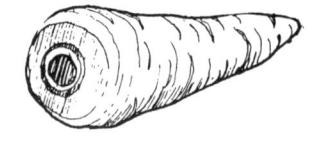

BAKED RABBIT

2 Jointed Rabbits
2 Eggs beaten well
4 ozs. Breadcrumbs

½ oz. Mixed Herbs
Sea Salt and pepper (freshly ground)

Coat the washed and dried joints with seasoned flour. Dip in the beaten eggs and coat with breadcrumbs and herbs; dot with butter. Place in a greased casserole and bake in the oven, removing at regular intervals to baste. Cook for two hours at 350°F.

"Aw loike a rabbit pie," wrote Lancashire dialect poet, Samuel Laycock in 1886, and an old recipe at that time was: Cut a rabbit into joints; wash and steep in water and salt for ten minutes. Remove as many of the large bones as possible and boil them in water. Line a deep pie dish with slices of ham and on this foundation lay the pieces of rabbit sprinkled with salt and the liver and kidneys. Add two hard-boiled eggs cut into slices and a cup of cold water. Bake in a moderate oven for an hour then place a pie crust over and bake for a further ½ hour, increasing oven temperature. Just before bringing to table carefully pour in through opening in pie crust the liquid in which the rabbit bones were cooked.

GROUSE OR PHEASANT PIE

1 grouse or pheasant
juice and rind of one lemon
1 oz butter
½ oz flour
chopped parsley

½ lb fillet of veal
¼ lb button mushrooms
¾ pint water
½ oz gelatine
1 oz dripping

FOR THE PASTRY CRUST

½ gill hot water
½ gill hot milk

6 ozs butter
¾ lb flour

FORCEMEAT BALLS

1 teacup breadcrumbs
grated lemon peel
1 egg

¼ onion
chopped parsley
½ oz suet

Cook the game and make the stock and gravy the day before. Put the grouse, veal and lemon peel in a double saucepan with cold water and cook for one hour. The stock from this later makes a rich brown gravy. Cut the meat into small pieces and reserve.

To make the gravy, melt the butter in a pan, add the flour, lemon juice and stock, stirring gently till it boils. Boil for two minutes and when it cools off, add the gelatine to dissolve slowly. Strain and leave till next day.

Chop the cooked liver of the bird and mix it with the ingredients listed for forcemeat balls. Shape mixture into small balls.

To make the pie crust, melt the butter in the milk and water and add it to the flour. Mix and knead the dough. Line the bottom of a deep pie dish with this pastry, rolled out, then line the sides of the dish and make a pastry lid. Glaze with beaten egg and bake placed on a baking sheet for 25 minutes in a moderate oven.

The pie, when cold, is filled with the cut up veal and grouse, the peeled and chopped mushrooms, forcemeat balls, parsley and cut up hard-boiled eggs, making layers. Use half of the gravy, put on the pastry lid again, which needs handling carefully, and bake for 20 minutes more. When cold, remove the lid and fill up with the remaining gravy which eventually forms a jelly.

This very old recipe recommends that the pie, when brought to table, "should be decorated with the head, feet, wings and some of the breast feathers", which strikes me as macabre, but it does indicate that plump game was once more readily procurable.

Instead of removing the pie lid, we would use a funnel or make a hole in the top in which to pour the gravy as in the recipe for Veal and Ham Pie.

A GOOD RABBIT PIE

Cut up the rabbit into several pieces. Soak in salt and water for half an hour. Stew for half an hour then place the pieces with thin layers of pork in a deep pie dish. Add a few slices of boiled egg. Sprinkle on a little pepper and nuts of butter. Pour in the water in which the rabbit was stewed. With a piece of bacon on top, bake in a hot oven for one hour, using puff pastry for the pie crust.

VEAL & HAM PIE

8 ozs self raising flour
5 ozs butter cut into pieces
12 ozs chopped ham
14 ozs chopped veal
3 tablespoons white wine

4 ozs mushrooms
½ pint vegetable stock
1 egg yolk
1 tablespoon milk
gelatine

Make the pastry by rubbing the butter into the flour and adding the wine. Place the smooth dough, rolled into a ball and wrapped with a tea towel, into the refrigerator for 20 minutes. Grease the pie dish, placing alternate layers of the ham, the veal and the chopped mushrooms, seasoned and sprinkled with dry parsley. Finish off with a layer of ham and pour in half of the stock. Quickly, and not handling it too much, roll the chilled pastry into a round, about ¼ ins. thick. Decorate with the remainder of the pastry cut into diamond or leaf shapes. Brush these with the beaten egg and milk and place on the pie lid. Brush more egg and milk mixture round the edges of the pie. Bake in a hot oven at 200°C. for one hour.

The jelly is made by softening the gelatine and adding the remaining vegetable stock. Heat gently till the gelatine has dissolved but do not boil. This liquid should be poured into the pie through a hole in the centre of the crust and the pie placed in a refrigerator to set.

A typical Sunday high tea dish, served with lots of fresh lettuce and tomatoes.

Snacks and Savouries

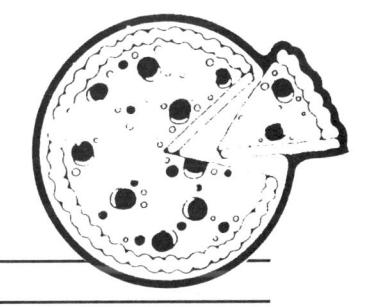

CHEESE AND POTATO PIE

1 lb potatoes
1 tablespoon thin cream
2 tomatoes and parsley
   for garnish
½ oz butter
2 ozs finely grated
   Lancashire cheese

Wash, peel and thickly slice potatoes, cover with cold water and boil until soft (15 minutes). Drain and mash them well. Add butter, cream, seasoning and beat in the finely grated cheese, setting aside a small portion. Spread the potatoes in a greased fireproof dish, sprinkling with the remaining cheese and thinly sliced tomatoes. Grill until golden brown and garnish with sprigs of parsley.

MACARONI CHEESE

Put 4oz of macaroni into a stewpan. Cover it with cold water, let it stand for an hour then bring it to the boil. Boil slowly till soft, after which drain through a colander. Melt in a stewpan 1½oz of butter with the same of flour. Add to it ½ pint of milk and a little salt. Stir till it boils then add the macaroni and mix well together. Have ready-grated 2 oz of cheese. Put a layer of prepared macaroni in a baking dish, then a layer of cheese, another layer of macaroni and so on, finishing on the top with grated cheese and morsels of butter placed here and there. Brown in the oven.

WELSH RAREBIT

Take one teaspoonful of mustard, half a cup of milk and a little salt. Put all in a saucepan. Add half a pound of mild cheese. Gently heat until thoroughly mixed and melted. Pour onto slices of toasted bread.

CHEESE STRAWS

8oz plain flour
2oz cheese, grated finely
egg yolk
4oz margarine
pinch of sea salt

Mix as you would pastry i.e. rubbing margarine into flour until it looks like breadcrumbs. Add grated cheese. Use the egg yolk to bind. Rollout and cut into strips. Bake for 20 minutes at 200°C.

CHEESE SOUFFLE

3 ozs cooking cheese
1 oz butter
½ oz flour

3 large eggs
¼ pint milk

Grease an oven-proof dish and grate the cheese. Separate the eggs. Melt the butter and stir in the flour, gradually adding the milk and bringing to the boil. Stir well to keep the mixture smooth. Cool. Add the cheese, egg yolks and some freshly ground pepper. Beat well. Whisk the egg whites until stiff and fold them into the cheese mixture. Place in the oven-proof dish and bake for 25 minutes in a moderate oven until well risen.

    Sure success with souffles is to allow them the oven to themselves.

SAVOURY EGGS

4 large free-range eggs
4 ozs Cheddar cheese
4 large slices tomato
4 tablespoons double cream

pinch of sea salt
freshly ground black pepper
water cress or parsley to garnish

Grate the cheese. Grease 4 ramekin dishes. Break an egg into each ramekin. Sprinkle cheese, salt and pepper on top. Cover with cream and place a slice of tomato on top. Cook for about 15 minutes in a moderate oven and serve when the eggs are set.

SAUSAGE AND EGG PIE

6oz plain flour
6oz sausage meat
2 hard-boiled eggs

3oz lard
2 tomatoes

Make short crust pastry with fat and flour. Line a flan tin. Smooth sausage meat all over the bottom of the tin. Slice tomatoes thinly and layer over sausage meat. Slice eggs and lay on top of tomato. Make a pastry lid and place on top. Bake in a hot oven 218°C for 10-15 minutes, then turn down to 180°C for another ¾ hour.

FLUFFY SCRAMBLED EGG

After sniffing winds blowing from Penyghent, walkers, potholers and railway enthusiasts visiting Ribblehead viaduct wolf with enthusiasm piles of scrambled egg on golden, wholemeal toast. The best results are undoubtedly obtained by cooking the eggs in a double saucepan.

Whip three or four free-range eggs with half a cup of milk, a sprinkle of herbs and crumbly Lancashire cheese. Place in the double saucepan containing a nut of butter and cook gently until the eggs rise set and fluffy. Use at once. Have the slices of toast buttered ready. If you don't cook this by water jacket but use an ordinary saucepan, gently "stroke" the mixture with a fork, smooth from the sides of the pan and watch it for about three minutes or until set and fluffy. Remove from heat at once. One minute extra and your eggs belong to the plastics industry and are ruined.

Invest if you can in a double saucepan. It is also invaluable for making trouble-free oatmeal porridge and lemon cheese.

SCOTCH EGGS

2 eggs
a small quantity of beaten egg
4 ozs sausage meat
parsley and green salad for garnish

Hard boil the eggs, cool and shell. Divide the sausage meat in half on a lightly-floured board and press into two rounds about 4 inches wide. Coat eggs with sausage meat, shaping neatly and taking care to keep the flour outside. Brush the coated eggs with beaten yolk and fry until the sausage meat is cooked. Drain well on kitchen paper and allow to cool.

RICH PANCAKES

2 ozs caster sugar
2 ozs melted butter
12 tablespoons flour
grated lemon peel (zest of lemon)
½ pint cream
4 eggs
1 tablespoon brandy

Mix cream, brandy, eggs, sugar and butter all together. Add the sifted flour very slowly, beating for a good 4 minutes. Prepare the pancakes in butter thus:

Melt a large lump in a pan until smoking hot then pour in a cup of the pancake mixture. The pancake should be cooked on both sides until brown. Fold each pancake up as you cook it and store in a hot, covered dish. When you have a pile ready pour over them a measured brandy with the grated lemon peel in it. This gives them a lovely flavour.

POTATO CAKES

Add 1 oz butter and 1 tablespoon chopped, cooked onion to 1 lb hot, mashed potato. Beat in 3-4 ozs flour. Roll out ¼ ins. thick, cut into rounds and fry until golden on both sides. Serve with grilled or fried sausages and baked beans. They are very good with a tin of Sainsbury's Ratatouille Provencale, which may be cheating but it is quick and tasty.

TOAD IN THE HOLE

½ lb sausages   ½ pint batter

Make the batter from 4 ozs plain flour, ½ pint milk and one egg. The milk should be added gradually and beaten well until the mixture is smooth and quite lump free.

Wash the sausages and remove from skins, place in a heat-proof dish and bake at 220°C. for ten minutes. Pour fat off the sausages and cover them with batter. Return to oven and bake for 40 minutes until risen and golden.

When my children were young they loved this as individual "toads", i.e. portions of sausage placed in patty tins and covered with the batter. Of course these cook more quickly so watch for the moment when they rise and turn golden brown.

BACON AND EGG PIE

8 ozs plain flour   a little water to bind
4 ozs cooking fat

Make this pastry in the usual way, rubbing fat into flour and binding together with a little water.

Filling is made from 2 rashers of bacon and 2 eggs with chopped onion and a sprinkle of herbs or chives. Seasoning to taste.

Roll out the pastry and line a flan dish. The bacon and onion should be cooked, eggs, herbs, milk and seasoning beaten up and the latter poured over the bacon and onions in the flan dish. Bake at 220°C. for 10 minutes then reduce heat to 175°C. for another ½ hour. An old recipe, now known by a fancy French name.

FRITTERS WITH BACON

3 tablespoonfuls flour
½ teaspoon baking powder
Pinch of salt and pepper

Add enough milk to make into a smooth paste. Take a tablespoonful of the mixture, drop into boiling fat and brown on both sides. These fritters are lighter than if made with eggs and as an extra flavour chopped comfrey leaves could be added to the paste before cooking. Many of the Victorian Fylde villas still have clumps of comfrey growing in their gardens.

MINCE FRITTERS

Allow to one pound of lean mince, one breakfast cup of bread crumbs and one egg. Beat the egg well and retain a little to dip the fritters in. Mix the rest in a bowl with the bread crumbs and mince, adding a teaspoon of mixed herbs or a chopped onion. Pepper and salt to taste. Form the mixture into small cakes about an inch thick, dip in flour and egg. Cook in melted dripping.

POTATO PIE

We adored this meal and never grew tired of it. Baked in the fireoven, Potato pie with a thick, brown crust was accompanied with freshly boiled young beetroot in vinegar, pickled red cabbage or pickled walnuts (all homemade and prepared by father).

1 lb. Stewing Steak
4 ozs. Chopped Onions
¾ pint Stock
1 dessertspoon Chopped Parsley

Salt and Pepper
2 lbs. Sliced Potato
1 lb. Pastry for Crust

Chop the meat into cubes; add the onions, stock, parsley, salt, pepper and put all into a deep, earthenware, pie dish; cover and slow cook in the oven for two hours, after which time remove the lid; cover with the thinly-sliced potatoes and pastry. Bake until well risen and brown, increasing oven temperature to 375°F.

SWEETBREADS STEWED

Lay the sweetbreads in salt and water for one hour. Wash thoroughly. Place in boiling water and boil for 10 minutes. Place them in cold water for a few minutes and trim neatly. Melt 2 ounces of butter in a saucepan and when quite hot, put in the sweetbreads, allowing them to stew gently for half an hour. Remove to a hot dish. Thicken the gravy with a little flour dissolved in half a teacup of milk. Bring to the boil, add pepper, salt and a teaspoonful of lemon juice. Pour this sauce over the sweetbreads.

SAVOURY FLAN

Line a tin or deep pie dish with pastry. Mince 4 ozs. cooked ham and onion. Add a pinch of sage and gently arrange the mixture in the uncooked pastry case. Skin a tomato by dropping it first into very hot water; cut it into slices and place it over the filling together with slices of hard-boiled egg. Sprinkle with chopped parsley. Beat one egg with one cup of milk and season it to taste. Pour this carefully and slowly over the mixture in the flan and bake in a moderate oven until set and nicely browned.

QUICHES

Cheesecakes and pastas have become very popular since more people have travelled abroad but they are only variations on original themes. Bought quiche is tasty but often has a wet bottom – unforgiveable in grandmother's day. A simple quiche can be made thus:

6 ozs. Shortcrust Pastry	¼ pint of Milk
2 ozs. Onion	2 tablespoons of Cream
4 ozs. Grated Lancashire Cheese	Salt and Pepper
4 ozs. Chopped Mushrooms	Chopped Parsley or Snipped Chives

Roll out the pastry and line a flan ring. Chop the onion finely and fry over gentle heat in butter till transparent. Gently cook the chopped mushrooms and arrange with the onions in the flan case. Whisk the eggs with the milk and cream; add the chopped parsley and spoon the mixture into the flan. Bake in centre of oven at 400°F. for 30 minutes, then reduce heat and bake for a further 10 minutes.

POTATOES SCONES

Take 2 cups of boiled, mashed potatoes, 1 cup of flour, 3 tablespoons of melted butter. Add the butter and as much flour as is needed; this varies according to the kind of potato, but don't make the mixture too dry. Brush with milk and brown under grill.

SQUIRE'S MUSHROOMS

2 ozs butter
½ red pepper diced
½ green pepper diced
2 ozs brown sugar
dash of Lea & Perrins sauce

1 lb button mushrooms
1 medium-sized onion diced
1 teaspoon Dijon mustard
4 fl. ozs red wine
salt and pepper

Melt the butter in a medium-sized saucepan. Add the red peppers, green peppers and onion. Sauté for about 2 minutes, without browning. Add the washed button mushrooms, sugar and mustard and stir for a further 4 minutes. Pour in the red wine, dash of Lea & Perrins, simmer for about 20 minutes. Season with salt and pepper according to taste.

This dish could be used as an appetiser or as a vegetarian dish, served with rice.

BOOTLE BRAISED RED CABBAGE

1lb red cabbage
1 medium or large onion
1 large cooking apple
1 clove garlic

1 teaspoon oregano
1 dessertspoon vinegar
1 dessertspoon sultanas

Finely shred the cabbage; peel and chop the onion. Peel and core apple and add sultanas, vinegar and crushed clove of garlic to a close-fitting saucepan greased inside with butter. Sweat gently for about 20-30 minutes, stirring often until contents are tender. Serve with Lancashire cheese or bacon if preferred.

COTTAGE CHEESE & SOUR CREAM STUFFED TOMATOES

8 ozs cottage cheese
6 medium tomatoes
2 ozs chopped celery
2 tablespoons mayonnaise or sour cream

½ teaspoon basil
minced celery leaves (for decoration)
2 tablespoons minced onion

Scoop out the pulp from the tomatoes. Mix all the ingredients together. Fill the tomatoes. Top with the minced celery leaves. Serve on a bed of lettuce.

STUFFED MARROW

4 ozs butter
1 medium marrow
1 large onion
2 ozs washed bran
1 teaspoon rubbed sage

½ pint chicken or vegetable stock
1 stick sound white celery
1 large Bramley apple
handful washed sultanas
seasoning of freshly ground peppercorns

Split the marrow after washing it and remove all the seeds. Into the hollow dot pieces of butter. Chop the celery and onion very fine. Add the bran, stock and seasoning. Simmer for 20 minutes, then add the sage, finely chopped apple and sultanas. Stuff both halves of the marrow with this mixture and put them side by side in a roasting tin. Dot more butter on top of each. Bake at 190°C. covered with foil for 1¾ hours, allowing 10 minutes at the end minus the foil.

    My family like this with mango chutney and extra, uncooked, sliced ripe tomatoes whose colour sets off this rather bland dish very well.

BLACKBURN CHEESE AND ONION PIE

Line a pie plate with pastry. Fill with small pieces of cheese and grated onion. (Chopping produces less tears – or use a blender.) Add seasoning and a very little milk, only enough to moisten the cheese and onion mixture. Cover with a pastry lid. Bake in a hot oven for about ½ hour and serve hot.

STUFFED TOMATOES

Use large, ripe tomatoes
½ lb. finely-minced, lean Steak
Onion, Parsley

1 teaspoon mixed, dried herbs and seasoning
Knobs of Butter
Left-over mashed Potato

Cut a slice from the top of each tomato. Remove seeds and scoop out some of the pulp; drain. Mix the meat, grated onion, chopped parsley, herbs and seasoning with the tomato pulp and carefully stuff the tomatoes with the savoury mixture. Place a layer of mashed potato over the top of each; dot with butter and bake in a moderate oven for 25 minutes. Sprigs of parsley or cress

CHEESE PUDDING

Break one egg. Mix it with 2 tablespoonfuls of milk and one of bread crumbs and ¼lb of grated cheese with ½oz of butter mixed in. Put in a mould and boil for 40 minutes or bake with bread crumbs and a scatter of nutmeg.

RICE RATATOUILLE

Use ½lb of brown rice and always soak it for an hour before cooking in 2 pints of salted water. Bring to boil and simmer for 45 minutes. Drain and rinse in warm water. Then prepare:

1 aubergine	1 onion
3 peeled tomatoes	1 green pepper
thyme	rosemary
seasoning	1 pint vegetable stock
1 clove of garlic	

Cut off the stem and small leaves of the aubergine. Wash and cut into cubes, discarding any coarse seeds. Slice the onion and pepper, pound the garlic, chop the tomatoes. Fry the onions and aubergines in butter for 5 minutes. Add pepper, garlic and tomatoes. Stir in the herbs and let the mixture simmer on, adding more stock to prevent burning. Stir these vegetables into the drained, hot rice. A sprinkle of finely grated cheese just before serving is a matter of choice.

This dish and Pizza are favourites with some members of the Liverpool Philharmonic Orchestra after a performance.

TURKEY OLIVES

4 turkey fillets
4 teaspoons wheat bran
1 teaspoon chopped parsley

1 egg
grated carrot

The stuffing:

4oz grated carrot
½ teaspoon grated orange rind
6 tablespoons cottage cheese

2 teaspoons wheat bran
grated nutmeg

Lay the turkey slices flat on a baking board and beat them flat and thin. Mix the stuffing ingredients together. Spread on the fillets of turkey and roll up each fillet. Beat the egg and brush it over the rolled-up fillets. Roll them in the bran. Impale the rolls on long skewers. Balance the skewers on the edges of a baking tin. Sprinkle the olives with corn oil and bake them at 180°C for 35 minutes. Serve the olives sprinkled with carrot and parsley.

ORIENTAL SALAD

2oz boiled, drained, long-grain rice
1 tablespoon chopped celery
1 tablespoon chopped cucumber
1 tablespoon chopped Chinese leaves
1 chopped, cored apple

1 tablespoon toasted chopped almonds
1oz raisins
2 hard-boiled eggs, halved
2 tablespoons mayonnaise
sprinkle of freshly ground sea salt

Mix the rice with the raisins, cucumber, celery and apple and place in a dish. Cut the eggs lengthwise, lay side down and place on the rice mixture. Cover with mayonnaise and sprinkle toasted almonds all over the salad. Serve very fresh.

Chutneys, Pickles & Sauces

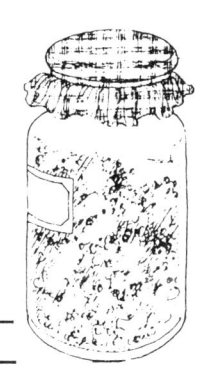

CHUTNEY

1 lb. Cooking Apples
1 teaspoon Sea Salt
1 lb. Green Tomatoes
1 lb. Onions
1 lb. Brown Sugar
2 pints White Vinegar

Peel and core the apples then chop them small with the onions and tomatoes. Pour on the vinegar, sugar and salt and stir it all up together. Cook until tender, stirring it at frequent intervals. Pot in clean jars or stoneware crocks and label.

Grandfather's pickled walnuts and red cabbage had a long preparation, committed to memory only. I recall the rows of green walnuts laid out in the sunshine, drying on the shed roof, and that he enjoyed this pickle with "collops" of best beef fried with onions.

PICKLED SAMPHIRE

Northern coast dwellers rave about pickled samphire. Although I have never tasted it myself, it sounds good, but not so if culled from a polluted coastline. If you find some growing fresh and clean (although much less plentiful, it still can be obtained on the salt marshes), this is what you do.

Wash it very well to remove all trace of grit or sand. Spread it out on a cloth in the sun and fresh air to dry. Put it in a pan with enough malt vinegar to cover the samphire and about one teaspoon of ground ginger. Allow it to boil until it changes colour and will slip off the stalk easily. Put it into jars and cover with vinegar. A prerequisite seems to be a true "sand grown" character to recognise the genuine article. In the old days samphire was gathered for sale in the towns and villages by country folk who had little other source of income. A Southport "sandgrounder" supplied the recipe.

PICKLED BEETROOT

Wash the beets, taking care not to prick or break any of the outside skin or fibres. Simmer in boiling water for –2 hours depending on size. Take out; allow to cool and slide skin off gently with the fingers. Slice and place in wide-mouthed jars. Boil vinegar and seasoning in the proportion of 2 ozs. whole pepper, 2 ozs. allspice to every gallon for ten minutes. Pour this liquid, when cold, onto the beets. Cover well.

APRICOT STUFFING

4 ozs dried washed apricots
1 large onion
4 ozs chopped walnuts
8 fl ozs white wine
8 ozs breadcrumbs
2 ozs butter

Soak the apricots in water overnight and on the second day soak them in the wine. Melt the butter over low heat and put in the chopped onion. Drain the wine from the apricots and keep it on one side whilst the fruit is chopped fine. Mix the apricots, walnuts, breadcrumbs and wine with the onion. If the stuffing is too mushy, add more breadcrumbs.

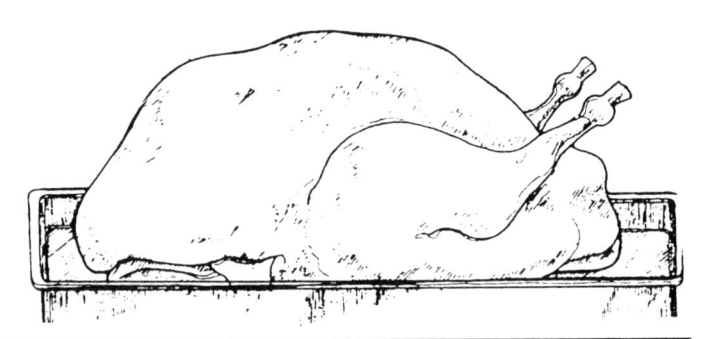

CRANBERRY SAUCE

Good home-made cranberry sauce can be prepared as follows:-

1 lb cranberries
1 dessert spoon cornflour
1 cup sugar
½ pint water

Wash the cranberries and put in a saucepan with water. Boil until soft. Rub them through a sieve, add sugar and reheat. With half a gill of cold water mix the cornflour and pour upon it the hot puree. Stir till it boils and allow five minutes to cook the cornflour.

GOOD BEEF STOCK

1 lb shin beef
1 lb raw bones, broken up
   by the butcher
4 pints cold water
2 carrots
2 onions
celery leaves
sprigs of parsley

Place the beef, cut into small pieces, into a pan with the bones. Add the water and bring to the boil. Peel and cut up the carrot, onion, parsley and celery leaves. Simmer the mixture very gently for four hours. Strain, cool, then keep in a refrigerator. The old-fashioned way was to boil vegetables in stock to retain their colour.

MINT JELLY

3lbs apples, preferably of the Bramley cooking type
1lb sugar to each pint of juice will be needed
4 tablespoons of very finely chopped mint leaves
green colouring
2 pints water
juice of 2 lemons
4 tablespoons, washed chopped mint leaves
4 tablespoons distilled malt vinegar

Wash and cut in halves the apples but there is no need to peel. Simmer in the water in a stainless steel pan until apples are soft. Strain through a sieve and measure the liquid, then boil it for 20 minutes with the chopped mint leaves (NOT the finely chopped). Strain again and use 1lb of sugar to each pint of liquid. Add lemon juice and vinegar. Stir well. Gently bring to boil. Boil briskly until a setting point is achieved. Stir in the finely chopped mint and a touch of green colouring. Pot and cover.

CHOW CHOW

1 quart small white onions
1 quart small cucumbers
1 quart vinegar
6 tablespoons mustard
1 tablespoon turmeric
2 heads cauliflower
3 green peppers
1 cup sugar
3 tablespoons flour

Peel onions and add cucumbers, cauliflower cut into small pieces and sliced peppers. Sprinkle with salt, cover with water and allow to stand overnight. Drain and cook in salted water until vegetables are tender and drain again. Boil vinegar in kettle (sic) or some suitable container and add paste made with mustard, flour, sugar, turmeric and a little cold vinegar, stirring until mixture thickens. Add vegetables and cook slowly for 10 minutes. Seal in sterilized jars.

TOMATO CATSUP

6 quarts tomatoes
3 tablespoons salt
1½ tablespoons black pepper
1 tablespoon allspice
½ cup brown sugar
½ tablespoon cloves
2 tablespoons cinnamon
1¼ cups vinegar

Remove stems from tomatoes and cut into small pieces. Put all ingredients together in a kettle (sic) i.e. a preserving pan and allow to simmer slowly until cooked down to one half. This takes about four hours. Stir occasionally to keep from burning. Strain. Pour into sterilized jars and seal. *"This is a highly seasoned sauce suitable for serving on meats or baked beans."*

BREAD SAUCE

Boil one medium onion stuck with cloves in a saucepan of 1½ cups of milk. Leave to stand for an hour. Strain off the liquid and mix it with six heaped tablespoons of white breadcrumbs. Return to heat; stir until thick and almost boiling. Add a teaspoon of butter and a tablespoon of cream when the mixture has cooled a little. Serve immediately with roast turkey or chicken.

EGG SAUCE

Boil three or four eggs until quite hard. Shell and chop them finely, then stir in melted butter. Season to taste with a little pepper and salt.

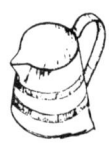

SWEET & SOUR SAUCE

1 dessertspoon Lea & Perrins or similar type of sauce
¼ pint water
2 slices pineapple with 4 tablespoons of the juice from the can
2 tablespoons malt vinegar
1oz brown sugar
2 tablespoons apple chutney
½oz cornflour

Put water, sugar, sauce and vinegar in a steel pan. Add the pounded-up pineapple and pickle. With the juice smooth in the cornflour to remove any lumps. Blend well and add to pan, stirring all the time. Bring to boil and simmer until cornflour is cooked (about 4 minutes).

ONION SAUCE

2 large onions, peeled, washed, sliced and cooked in boiling water until tender. Drain well. Add sea salt from a mill, about 1 tablespoon of butter and chop well. This sauce looks and tastes very good with lamb cutlets or well-browned sausages.

WINTER MINT

Gently warm a pot of runny honey. Wash and chop the leaves of a bunch of mint. Layer mint with honey in a jar in proportion of $\frac{1}{4}$ inch mint $\frac{3}{4}$ inch honey. Cover well and store in a cool place. Thus winter mint sauce can be made by mixing 2 tablespoons of mint and honey to $\frac{1}{4}$ pint of pure malt vinegar.

GAME JELLY

1 cupful of cold game
juice of 2 large oranges
1 pint stock
1 onion
1 orange to garnish
2 teaspoons meat extract to enrich stock
1 hard-boiled egg
$\frac{3}{4}$ oz gelatine

The stock can be made by boiling the carcase of the bird with an onion. Simmer, after bringing to the boil, until there is a pint of liquid available. Soak the gelatine in the orange juice for 15 minutes then add it to the stock and strain. Chop the cup of game with a half teaspoon of mixed herbs or fresh snipped chives. Pour half a cup of the mixture into a mould. Allow to set and decorate with slices of hard-boiled egg. Gradually pour on more, allowing to set until all the mixture is used.

SLOE AND APPLE JELLY

2lb sloes
2lb cooking apples
1lb of brown sugar to every pint of juice
2 pints of water
Pinch of spice

Put the sloes into a preserving pan. Chop the apples. Place together and pour in the water. Bring the contents slowly to the boil then reduce to a simmer, stirring frequently for about one hour. The fruit pulp must be strained through a jelly bag and the juice collected in a bowl beneath. Return juice to pan and bring it to the boil. Stir in the sugar until dissolved and boil until setting is reached. Pour into warmed jars and cover when cold. This was evidently a favourite with the scones recipe. Jelly made from rowan berries was served with pheasant.

RHUBARB JELLY

To make rhubarb jelly wash and wipe dry some fresh, red rhubarb, but do not peel. Cut up and put into preserving pan with one cupful of water. Simmer gently, allowing juice to flow, then strain through a jelly bag. To each large cupful of juice allow 1lb lump sugar. Stir gently until it boils and boil for ten minutes at least. Pour into small pots, seal and store in cool, dry place.

ROSEMARY SYRUP

2 pints of water
A handful of rosemary
Sugar

Pour the boiling water onto the chopped rosemary and leave to stand overnight. Strain the liquid next day and to each pint of liquid add 1lb of sugar. Boil until syrupy. Allow to cool. Bottle. It was evidently a soothing, sore throat remedy.

GOOSEBERRY CHUTNEY

2lb brown sugar
1lb raisins
2oz ground ginger
2oz mustard
$\frac{1}{40}$oz cayenne pepper

$\frac{1}{4}$lb garlic
$\frac{1}{4}$lb salt
2lb sour apples or gooseberries
3 pints malt vinegar

The garlic, raisins and apples (or gooseberries) to be boiled in the vinegar till soft then put through a sieve. The other ingredients to be added and all boiled up.

COLE SLAW

Shred the heart of a firm Savoy cabbage very finely and cover with the following dressing:
    Whisk two eggs in a jug with two tablespoons of milk and two tablespoons of brown sugar, ½ teaspoon of Pommery or plain mustard and a little sea salt, 8 ozs. of white vinegar and water. Stir constantly. Pour into the jug two tablespoons of melted butter; keep stirring over heat until the dressing thickens. Do not pour over the shredded cabbage until quite cold.

HERB PUDDING

"We will have herb pudding and sit in the sun."

This Ribble Valley recipe is very old and similar to one I was given in Bavaria at a very old inn. The Germans used chopped white turnip tops instead of spinach. My son, who speaks fluent German, was able to translate, but I was most impressed by the similarity of these old country recipes. Outside Beatrix Potter books, I never believed herb pudding really existed.

4 ozs wholemeal flour
4 ozs oatmeal
2 ozs spinach, spring cabbage
  or young nettles - chopped
4 ozs shredded suet
2 teaspoons chopped, mixed herbs

Mix all together with a little watery milk to make a fairly stiff dough but not sticky so add the liquid very carefully. Put into a well-greased pudding basin and cover with greaseproof paper or boiled muslin cloth. Steam for 3 hours.

    This pudding can be used instead of potatoes with meat or savouries. It can even be sliced cold and fried in dripping. What was once a poor agricultural labourer's dish may well now be regarded as a luxury starter for the fibre-conscious.

GREEN TOMATO CHUTNEY

1lb green tomatoes
½lb onions
1½ pints malt vinegar
½lb brown sugar
5oz seedless raisins
1½lb peeled, cored cooking apples
1oz pickling spice in a muslin bag

Mince the fruit and vegetables as finely as possible. Place in a steel pan with the bag of spice, vinegar, sugar, raisins and boil all gently for two hours. Pot as before.

CELERY AND TOMATO CHUTNEY

2lb ripe tomatoes
1 large celery
1lb onions
8oz brown sugar

¼ teaspoon allspice
½ teaspoon dry mustard
1 pint malt vinegar

Skin the tomatoes by dropping them into boiling water. Chop finely. Wash the celery and chop finely. Peel, wash and chop finely the onions. Put all ingredients into a stainless steel pan. Bring to boil and simmer slowly for 1½-2 hours or until mixture thickens well. Pour into hot jars and seal.

It is advisable to keep the kitchen door well closed in chutney making, otherwise the house gets permeated with malt vinegar scents.

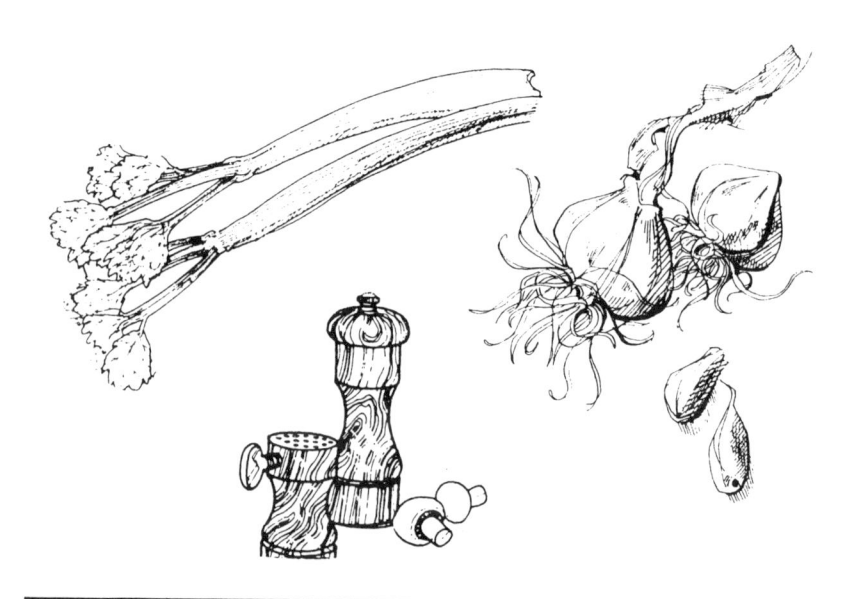

RHUBARB AND DATE CHUTNEY

1lb cooking dates
1lb onions
½oz mixed spice tied
  in a muslin bag

3lbs rhubarb
1lb soft brown sugar
1 pint malt vinegar
salt and pepper

Wash rhubarb and cut into short pieces. Wash and chop dates. Peel the onions and slice. Put all ingredients into a pan and simmer until a thick consistency is arrived at. Take out and discard the muslin bag. Pot the chutney in warm, clean jars and tie down securely, labelling if you have other chutneys in the store cupboard.

Invalid Foods

EGG FLIP

Break a fresh, free-range egg into a cup. Add one or two tablespoonfuls of milk and a little brown sugar. Beat until frothy. Strain into a tumbler and serve.

Milk and milk drinks are good if the invalid will tolerate them. So are freshly squeezed fruit juices, especially lemonade made from fresh fruit. Rosehip syrup, barley water and consomme soups are also suitable, but do not press anything if the invalid does not fancy it. Ray knobs cooked in milk with seasoning make a light, nourishing lunch. Eggs, white meat and light sponge puddings or finger biscuits are fairly easy to digest, but avoid all fried foods, very new bread, fatty foods, heavy cheese and NEVER re-heat foods. The latter is a good rule all the time. Lots of fluids, love and patience work wonders.

STEAMED EGG

1 Egg
½ oz. Butter
1 tablespoon of Milk
¼ teaspoon of Salt
1 pinch of Pepper

Grease a cup well with the butter; add the milk; break the egg and drop it in, sprinkling over with seasoning. Place the cup in a saucepan and pour round, enough boiling water to come up half way. Boil slowly for ten minutes; turn the egg out onto a hot plate and serve at once.

OATMEAL PORRIDGE

¼ cup of Medium Oatmeal
1 cup of Water
Pinch of Sea Salt

Boil the water in a saucepan and as it comes to the boil, stream in the oatmeal, stirring all the time. Cover and simmer gently for ten minutes, then add the salt and stir well. Simmer for another ten minutes. Serve hot in individual bowls of cold milk with a sprinkling on top of Demerara sugar or raw cane sugar.

CHICKEN BRAWN

3½ lbs. Boiling Fowl
2 Pigs' Trotters
2 hard-boiled Eggs

Mixed Herbs
Sea Salt and Pepper

Place the fowl in a pan with the trotters, salt, pepper and mixed herbs. Cover with water and bring to the boil. Remove to the oven. In a large, lidded, ovenware dish, it can then be cooked at 300°F for four hours. When cool, strip off all meat from chicken and trotters, chop finely, taste a morsel to be sure seasoning balance is correct. Return the meat to the liquid and heat through. Line a wet, deep dish with the sliced, hard-boiled eggs and gently pour in the meat, pressing down well. Leave to cool; cover with a sheet of greaseproof paper, then press under a weight for several hours. When set, it can be turned out, garnished with watercress and sliced up for a family meal.

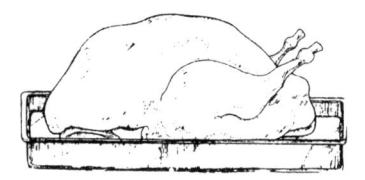

CHICKEN BROTH

Joint the fowl. Put in a saucepan and cover with cold water. Boil gently for ¾ hour then add a dessertspoonful of rice, finely chopped parsley and seasoning (sea salt, celery salt, pepper). Boil for another half hour; skim and serve with squares of toast.

TREACLE POSSET

A teaspoonful of treacle stirred into a teacupful of warm milk is good for a cold. A teaspoonful of honey stirred into warm milk is very good for getting an excitable child off to sleep.

BARLEY WATER

Boil half a teacup of pearl barley in one breakfast cup of cold water. Let it simmer gently for half an hour. Pare the yellow rind thinly off a fresh lemon and put it into a jug. Strain the barley water into the jug and let it infuse for ten minutes with a lid or piece of paper over the jug. It is then ready for drinking.

LEMON AND HONEY

Pour hot water over a tablespoonful of honey in a beaker. Add the juice of two or three lemons. Drink at regular intervals to soothe and heal a sore throat. For the same purpose use Raspberry Vinegar.

BEEF TEA

One pound of lean Shin Beef and one pint of cold water. Chop the beef finely and add to the water. Bring slowly to boiling point. Place all in a stone jar, tying a clean cloth tightly over the top. Place this jar in a pan of water which covers it within an inch of the top. Simmer slowly for three hours, replenishing water as necessary. Half a teacupful of pearl barley can also be added if desired.

This old recipe, a great standby in our house in the 20's and 30's, is now declared by some authorities to have little nutritional value. The way my mother made it (cooked slowly on the hob) brought out a delicious flavour and we four children clamoured for it, ill or well. Beef stew with a cowheel was another so-called "strengthener".

NED FEELEN'S BUN LOAVES

2 lbs. Plain Flour
4 ozs. Margarine
3 ozs. Currants
1 oz. Mixed Peel
2 ozs. Yeast

4 ozs. Sugar
1 teaspoon Salt
3 ozs. Sultanas
1 Egg
1 pint Milk and Water

Rub the margarine into the flour. Add the sugar, salt, currants, sultanas and peel. Make a well in the centre. Put in the yeast mixed with a little water and the whole egg. Stir in half of the warm milk and water and allow to stand for ten minutes. Knead to a light dough, using the remainder of the milk and water, and allow to stand again for ten minutes. Put into two, warmed, greased tins and allow to rise for twenty minutes. Bake in a moderate oven for about half an hour. When baked, brush over with sugar and milk to glaze.

In grandmother's day, the dough was placed in a large earthenware bowl, cream glazed inside, and set upon the warm hearthstone to rise.

Puddings and Pies

CUSTARD PUDDING

3 tablespoonfuls of Flour
3 Eggs
3 breakfast cupfuls of Milk

Put the flour into a bowl and make into batter with a little cold milk. Separate the yolks from the whites of eggs. Put the whites on a flat plate and beat to a froth with a flat, open-wire beater. Beat the yolks also and add them to the batter. Put the remainder of the milk in a saucepan to warm a little; add the batter and sugar to taste. Stir well till it boils. Boil for four minutes then lift off heat to cool a while. Add the whites, stirring them in lightly to keep froth on top. A drop of vanilla flavouring at this point is optional. The heat of the pudding cooks the whites sufficiently and gives a lovely texture to a nourishing, light pudding.

MARTHWAITE BAKED CUSTARD

1 pint Milk
4 tablespoons of Sugar
4 Egg Yolks

Vanilla to flavour
Nutmeg

The yolks and sugar should be beaten together and the milk boiled. Whilst still boiling pour over the yolk mixture and keep stirring. Turn into a large, buttered dish after straining. Bake in a moderate oven for 25 minutes. Sprinkle with the grated nutmeg. The mixture can be baked in a pastry case to form custard pie.

MANCHESTER PUDDING

¾ pint milk
pinch of salt
rind of ½ lemon
yolks of 2 eggs
2oz sugar
3oz breadcrumbs
1oz butter

3 tablespoons pineapple jam mixed with 1 tablespoon rum OR 3 tablespoons apricot jam mixed with 1 tablespoon sherry.

Also, to make the meringue you will need 2 egg whites and 2oz caster sugar.

Pour warmed milk flavoured with lemon rind over breadcrumbs. Add yolks of eggs, sugar, salt, melted butter. Pour into buttered pie dish standing in a pan of warm water. Bake at 180° until firm. When baked, spread with jam and wines (optional). Pile meringue on top and bake again at 150°C until golden brown.

HALF-PAY PUDDING

¼lb suet
¼lb breadcrumbs
¼lb raisins
3 tablespoons treacle
¼lb currants
1 teaspoon baking powder
¼lb flour
a little milk

Mix together and steam for 1½ hours.

STRAWBERRY JAM PUDDING

4oz margarine
4oz caster sugar
milk to mix
8oz S.R. flour
2 eggs
5 tablespoons home-made strawberry jam

Place the jam at the bottom of a large, greased pudding basin. Cream the margarine and sugar. Beat in the eggs. Fold in flour and add about 1½ tablespoons of milk. Pour this mixture into pudding basin and cover with foil. Steam for at least two hours. This is a lovely winter pudding to remind you of summer. We like it with plain white sauce. As a variant you could leave out jam and flavour the sponge mixture with lemon, orange or chocolate.

SAVOURY FRUITY PUDDING

A savoury to be fried and accompanied with bacon.

9oz breadcrumbs
4oz flour
2oz sugar
3oz currants
2oz sultanas
1 level teaspoon of cinnamon
¼ pint milk

Mix the ingredients all together (fruit last) to form a dough. Pack it well down into a loaf tin. Cover and steam for 2 hours. Cool completely. (Chilling is better and any unused can be frozen). The slices should be quickly fried and served with bacon and eggs.

POOR MAN'S PUDDING

½ cup chopped suet
½ cup currants
1 cup flour
½ cup brown sugar
½ cup seeded raisins
1½ cups grated old bread
2 teaspoons baking powder
2 cups milk

Mix ingredients in the order given. Beat well. Put into a greased mould. Place in covered saucepan with boiling water half way up the sides of the mould. Steam for 2 hours. Turn out carefully. This was served with:

PINEAPPLE PUDDING

4 ozs butter
4 ozs self raising flour
4 ozs caster sugar
4 ozs golden syrup
2 large eggs
pineapple

Line an 8 ins. square tin and pour the warmed golden syrup into the bottom. Arrange slices of pineapple on top (if tinned variety used it should be well drained). The creamed mixture which goes on top of this is made by the usual method. Bake for an hour at 150°C. until golden brown and firm to touch. Serve with custard.

EVE'S PUDDING

The name suggests apples but any fruit or good home-made jam can be substituted.

4 ozs self raising flour	1 lb baking apples
4 ozs butter	lemon juice and rind
4 ozs caster sugar	2 eggs

Peel and core apples. Slice and place in pie dish in layers with sugar and lemon juice. Cream the flour, butter, sugar and eggs together and pour this mixture onto the fruit. Bake for about one hour at 150°C. until sponge is a firm, golden brown. By then the apples will be well cooked.

RICE PUDDING

The most important rule about rice pudding is not to buy it in a tin. There's no need for this sound, body-building food, properly made, to be at all boring. As an accompaniment to stewed apples or laced with rose hip syrup it's very good fare indeed.

Wash two tablespoonsfuls of pudding rice. Add one tablespoonful of brown sugar. (This makes the milk look appetisingly creamy.) Pour on a pint of milk and scatter ground nutmeg on the surface. Bake in a very moderate oven for 1½ hours until nicely "creeded".

TOFFEE PUDDINGS

6 small sponge buns	1 tablespoonful finely
6 slices of pineapple	chopped nuts
(preferably fresh)	glace cherries
1 lemon	

You will need, to make the toffee:

¼ lb butter or margarine	½ lb golden syrup
¼ lb brown sugar	

Each sponge bun should be soaked with pineapple and lemon juice, which takes a tablespoonful. Melt the margarine and golden syrup over gentle heat. Add the sugar and boil carefully for 15 minutes. Stir till you feel it thicken and pour a spoonful over each bun. Decorate with nuts and cherries and slices of pineapple.

COTTAGE PUDDING

1 teacupful flour
½ teacupful sugar
3 ozs butter or margarine
rind of a lemon, grated
1 teaspoonful baking powder

Rub margarine into flour. Add sugar, baking powder and grated lemon rind. Mix with milk to a stiff dough. Bake in a greased pie dish in a moderate oven for 45 minutes.

FRUITY PUDDING

10 ozs mixed dried fruits
(currants, sultanas, raisins)
2 cups water
1 cup golden syrup
pinch of nutmeg
¼ cup tapioca

Simmer the dried fruit in the water for half an hour. Drain, reserve liquid and fruit and make up liquid to 2 cups. Add syrup. Combine tapioca and nutmeg and stir into the liquid. Allow to stand 5 minutes. Bring to boil, stirring well. Allow to stand until thickened. Pour half the mixture into a dish and spread the fruit on top. Cover with rest of tapioca mixture. Cool. Serve with a thin, plain sauce.

FLORRIE'S FRUIT SPONGE

Use any fruit in season, washed and sweetened with sugar. Place in a dish, then take:

4 tablespoons S.R. flour
2oz margarine
1 egg
3 tablespoons sugar
a little milk

Cream the sugar and margarine. Add flour, egg and milk alternately until you achieve a soft mixture, then pour over fruit in basin and bake at 180°C until risen and golden brown.

CARROT PUDDING

½lb stoned raisins
½lb currants
½lb boiled grated carrots
½lb suet
¼lb sugar
2oz candied peel
½lb breadcrumbs

Enough flour to mix it to a moderately stiff paste. Butter a mould or basin. Put in the mixture and boil for four hours.

FIG PUDDING

½lb bread crumbs
½lb figs
6oz suet
6oz sugar

Figs and suet to be finely minced. Add 2 eggs well beaten and a little nutmeg. Boil for 4 hours in a well-buttered, covered basin, after stirring well into this mixture, the bread crumbs and sugar.

This is very good with the recipe for apricot sauce.

SLOW PANCAKES

This new, slower to make, recipe blends together two eggs, ½ pint of milk, ½ pint of water, 2 tablespoonfuls of melted butter, 3 ozs. of flour and a pinch of salt. The batter is then left to stand for an hour. A small, clean frying pan should be brushed with melted butter and a dessertspoon of the batter dropped in. Tilt the pan to spread it evenly; brown lightly and quickly over high heat. A heated dish can be filled with the pancakes, caster sugar dusted between layers, more melted butter poured over and finished off with a glass of brandy.

The ancient market town of Poulton-le-Fylde still rings the Pancake Bell on Shrove Tuesday. Traditionally it was rung by an apprentice to call the other apprentices from work and "prepare to eat their pancakes", which were begged from house to house in the village. The boy who ate the most pancakes was a champion.

ARLOUISE'S GINGER SPONGE

2 breakfast cups Flour
1 breakfast cup Sugar
1 teacup Milk
1 tablespoon Treacle
1 teaspoon Bicarbonate of Soda

1 tablespoon Syrup
1 teaspoon Ginger
1 tablespoon Butter
1 Egg

Rub the butter into the flour; add sugar, ginger, treacle, syrup. Beat up the egg; add it with the milk and stir well. Put the bicarb of soda in a tablespoon of boiling water and add to mixture whilst still fizzing. Beat the mixture for five minutes. Bake in a moderate oven for ¾ hour and serve with white sauce.

LEMON DELIGHT

2 ozs. Butter
4 ozs. Caster Sugar
1 Lemon

1 Egg
2 level tablespoonfuls Plain Flour
¼ pint Milk

Cream the sugar and butter. Stir in the lemon juice and grated lemon rind. Add the egg yolk. Stir in the flour and the milk. Whip the egg white stiffly and fold into the mixture. Pour into a greased 1 pint pie dish and stand the dish in a tray of cold water. Bake in a very moderate oven for one hour.

PINEAPPLE PUDDING

2 ozs. Butter
2 ozs. Plain Flour
½ pint Milk
2 ozs. Sugar

2 Eggs
1 small tin Pineapple or better still, fresh pineapple crushed
4 ozs. Caster Sugar for the meringue

Melt the butter; add the flour and cook until the mixture leaves the side of the pan. Add the milk gradually, stirring all the time to make a thick sauce. Cool slightly. Stir in the sugar, egg yolks and pineapple juice. Reheat the sauce until it thickens again, stirring all the time. Chop the pineapple and put it into a greased pie dish. Cover with the pineapple sauce.

To make the meringue, beat the egg whites until stiff; add half the caster sugar. Beat again until the meringue stands up in peaks. Fold in the rest of the caster sugar. Cover the pineapple with the meringue and sprinkle with caster sugar. Cook in a slow oven until the meringue is crisp.

FRUIT CRUMBLE

1 lb. Soft Fruit (e.g. apples, plums)
5 ozs. Plain Flour
5 ozs. Sugar

3 ozs. Butter
3 ozs. Sugar

Stew the fruit with the 5 ozs. of sugar and allow to cool; pour into a heatproof dish. Rub the butter into the flour and stir in the 3 ozs. of sugar. Spread the mixture over the fruit. Bake in a moderately hot oven.

BARBER GREEN PUDDING

½ pint Milk
2 ozs. Sugar
1 oz. Butter
2 Eggs

Breadcrumbs (Reduce about half of a small loaf)
3 tablespoons Strawberry Jam
Cinnamon

Boil the milk, butter and sugar and pour over the breadcrumbs, egg yolk and scattering of cinnamon. Place in a greased pie dish and bake in a slow oven until set. Spread with the warmed jam. Beat the egg whites until stiff; fold in 1 oz. of caster sugar and pour onto the top of the pudding. Place in the oven to brown the delicious meringue topping. This is a lovely, light, summer pudding, improved further with a few fresh strawberries tossed into each serving.

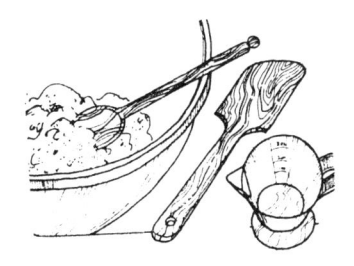

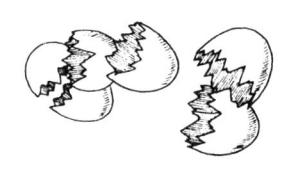

LEMON (OR GINGER) PUDDING

A light Lemon Pudding doubles in cooler weather as Ginger Pudding, as the lemon and ginger flavours are interchangeable.

Butter the mould and ornament it with raisins. Take:

½lb breadcrumbs
½lb flour
½lb loaf sugar

Juice of two lemons
Glass of sherry
1 egg

Mix all up together and steam for 3 hours. Can be served with arrowroot sauce with a little sherry in it or with . . .

LEMON SAUCE

1 teaspoonful of cornflour
Rind of half a lemon

Sugar to taste
Juice of half a lemon with a little water

Put the rind in cold water to boil then add cornflour, sugar and juice.

MARY ANNE'S PUDDING

> *One good teacupful of flour; the same of sugar*
> *2 eggs and 2oz of butter*
> *½ teaspoonful of carbonate of soda and the same of cream of tartar*
> *Season with nutmeg and cinnamon*

Well butter the mould and before pouring in batter, place two tablespoonfuls of jam in the top. A little milk may well be added to the eggs. Boil for two hours. Quantities may be doubled to produce a larger pudding. Mary Anne gave no instructions as to how to make the "batter". I creamed the butter and sugar, added the flour and raising agents, the beaten eggs, spices and a little thin cream.

ROSY APPLES IN SYRUP

Six large, rosy apples, washed but not peeled. Remove the core from the base of the apple, retaining the stalk. Dissolve 2 ozs. of sugar in ½ pint of water to make the syrup. Put the apples with 3 tablespoonfuls of plum or raspberry jam into a casserole, then pour over the syrup and juice of a lemon. Stew gently till tender but whole. Lift the apples onto a hot dish; strain the syrup over them and scatter with blanched, shredded almonds.

VALLEY APPLE PUDDING

> *3 Eggs and the weight of these 3 eggs in Flour, Sugar and Butter*

Cream the butter and sugar. Beat in the eggs, gradually at the same time adding the flour. Place well-chopped apples at the base of a large pudding basin and cover with the mixture. Steam for 2½ hours. Serve with custard. It is useful to have extra "dollops" of apple ready for those who complain they haven't got enough fruit.. I make an extra saucepanful. Bramleys are ideal, gently stewed with brown sugar sufficiently long for them to "fall". Don't overcook. They can be kept warm under the hob in a fire-proof dish. The Valley refers to Rossendale where my mother was born.

Using the same mixture with a fistful of sultanas and currants added, arranged in individual bun tins and cooked for about twenty minutes in a moderate oven, will produce delicious fruit buns for tea or supper.

PLUM FRITTERS

1 pint milk
1lb plain flour
1 packet vanilla sugar
1 egg
1 teaspoon baking powder
1lb plums

Mix the flour, baking powder and vanilla sugar together with a pinch of cooking salt. Beat in the egg and milk gradually, taking the flour from the sides of the bowl. Wash and stone the plums. Cut in half. Give the batter a further good beating. It should be thick enough to coat the back of a wooden spoon. Then drop spoonfuls of it into hot, deep fat half way up a well-buttered frying pan. Place a half plum in each fritter. Sprinkle with sugar when cooked a golden brown after draining well on layers of kitchen roll paper.

Apple, peeled halved bananas and pineapple fritters can be made in much the same way. Tinned pineapple should be well drained. The apples should be cored, peeled and sliced into rings. Dip each ring of fruit into the batter and carefully lower into the hot fat. To test whether the fat is hot enough for fritters, drop a cube of white bread into it; the bread should turn golden brown very quickly.

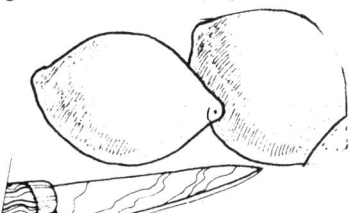

PORCUPINE PIPPINS

Grandmother could make this dish for fourpence, old money.

½ lb dried apples
2 ozs almonds
rind and juice of a lemon
2 cloves
4 ozs sugar
peach or apricot jam

Cover the apples with boiling water and let them soak for 10 hours. Cook them gently in the water, putting in the cloves, thinly pared lemon rind and the sugar. Put the apples in a dish after about half an hour, but let the liquid simmer on and reduce itself. Blanch the almonds by pouring boiling water over them and slipping off the brown skins. With a sharp knife slice the almonds into strips. Carefully fill the apples with the jam and pour the syrup from the pan over each. Stick the slivers of almonds all over the apples. The porcupines are good with either cream or natural yoghurt.

Nowadays it's not so easy to get dried whole apples, but it's worth looking ahead and storing a small, pippin variety. Peel when they become wizened and treat as above. They make a nice change from the straight-forward baked Bramley and children enjoy the novelty.

CUP PUDDING

1 teacupful of flour
1 teacupful breadcrumbs
1 teacupful sultanas
1 teacupful suet (shredded)
1 teacupful milk
1 teacupful sugar
½ teaspoonful of carbonate of soda
1 teaspoonful of cinnamon

Mix well and boil for three hours.

STRAWBERRY PIE

1 cup flour	*4 tablespoons butter*
½ teaspoon salt	*¼ cup cold water*
2 teaspoons baking powder	*1 quart strawberries*

Sift dry ingredients together; rub in butter very lightly with finger tips; add water slowly to make a stiff dough. Roll out on floured board and use for bottom crust of pie, being careful to fold the pastry well over the edge of pie plate. Bake in hot oven 12 to 15 minutes. If glazed crust is desired, brush edges after baking with boiling hot syrup (2 tablespoons syrup and 1 tablespoon water) and return to oven for 1 or 2 minutes until syrup hardens. Fill the baked crust with fresh selected hulled strawberries and cover with syrup made as follows: Add ½ cup sugar and ½ cup strawberries to 2 cups boiling water; bring to a boil and strain; add 1 tablespoon corn starch which has been mixed with little cold water. Cook over hot fire for a minute or two, stirring constantly; remove from fire and beat hard; return to slow fire, cook very gently until thick. Pour while hot over strawberries. Serve either hot or cold.

QUEEN OF JAM PIES

This is queen because of the jam, made every September from equal quantities of yellow egg plums and Victoria plums. It has a full pie crust slapped upon a generous amount of this delicious jam, the pie being cooked in a hot oven until browned, which takes 20 minutes. Over-cooking is anathema as this will "toffee" the jam, which should essentially keep its jelly texture and delicate flavour.

JAM

6 lbs ripe Victoria plums
8 lbs preserving sugar
6 lbs ripe yellow egg plums

Halve the plums. Take out as many stones as possible. Crack a number of the stones and skin the kernels. Spread the fruit in a large bowl and sprinkle with half the sugar. Leave for 24 hours. Put the fruit and syrupy juice into a preserving pan and cook gently until the fruit is soft. Add the remaining sugar and kernels. Bring to the boil until a little of the jam will set on a cold plate. Do not overboil.

PASTRY

4 ozs lard
9 ozs flour
1 dessertspoon sugar

Working quickly and lightly with cold hands, rub the fat into the flour until it resembles large breadcrumbs. Add the sugar. Sprinkle in a tablespoon of water, lightly stirring and tossing the mixture with a fork until the mixture is evenly distributed. Add as little water as is necessary to make the pastry hold together under light pressure. It is then ready for rolling out, using only gentle pressure on the lightly floured board and rolling pin. Lift and turn the pastry occasionally to make sure it is not sticking to the board. Roll as thinly as possible. Line a pie dish, add the jam and cover with a pastry lid.

MRS ANDERSON'S CAKE

6 eggs
Their weight in sugar, flour and half their weight in butter
1½ teaspoons of baking powder
3 tablespoonfuls of milk

Beat butter and sugar well, adding one egg at a time until they are all used, then mix baking powder well with the flour and add the other ingredients, last of all the milk. Bake in a moderate oven. This quantity will make two nice cakes which can be clapped together with raspberry jam and dusted with sugar.

AN 1860 "DELICIOUS DISH OF APPLES"

Boil ½lb of sugar in a pint of water for 20 minutes, then add 2lb of apples, pared and cored, with the juices and a little of the peel of 2 small lemons. Boil this mixture until quite stiff. Put into two moulds and turn out when cold.

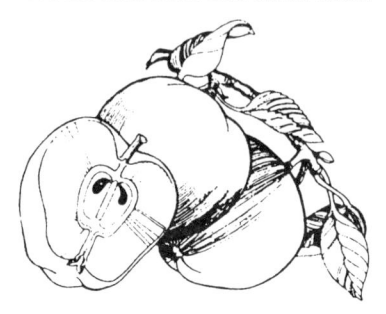

VERY GOOD TREACLE TART

Cover with short pastry the middle of a soup plate. Pour thickly over it some treacle with fine bread crumbs added. Cover with pastry and bake immediately in a hot oven.

TREACLE PUDDING

Mix in a basin one teacupful each of finely chopped suet, bread crumbs and flour. Add half a pound of treacle, a dessertspoonful of sugar, a teaspoonful of milk, half a teaspoonful of carbonate of soda. Stir so that the ingredients are thoroughly mixed. Put into a buttered mould and steam for two and a half hours.

PINEAPPLE DELIGHT

Bring ¾ pint of milk to boiling point and stir in 2oz of semolina. Cook for a few minutes, pour into a basin and add 4oz of fresh pineapple thinly sliced.

> 4oz honey
> 4oz breadcrumbs
> The juice and finely chopped rind of half a lemon
> 1 teaspoonful ground ginger
> 2oz butter and 3 yolks of eggs

Mix and then lightly fold in the whites of 3 eggs, well beaten. Steam in a buttered mould for an hour and serve on a hot dish with extra pineapple juice.

PLUM PUDDING

1lb bread crumbs	6 eggs
1lb raisins	4oz butter
1lb currants	1lb sugar
1 pint milk	Cinnamon, ginger, nutmeg

It is best to mix this pudding the day before it is wanted.

Pour the boiling milk over the bread crumbs, cover with a plate and allow to stand for an hour. Then add currants, raisins, sugar and butter, half a teaspoonful of cinnamon, the same of ginger and nutmeg and last, add eggs well beaten (break each egg separately into a cup before adding to others). Mix as for cake baking, bringing the spoon from the outside; never stir in the centre. Put in a buttered mould, cover and boil steadily for five hours. On no account must the pudding get off boiling point. Serve with a sweet sauce.

KISS ME QUICK

To 2oz fresh butter beaten to a cream, add 2oz of sifted sugar and gradually stir in 2oz of flour and one teaspoonful of baking powder. Lastly add 2 well-beaten eggs and 2 tablespoonfuls of raspberry jam. Beat all thoroughly together. Put in a buttered mould and steam for two hours.

This light, golden pudding needs only a plain cornflour sauce to set off its delicate flavour.

Strangely enough we found that a portion of pudding warmed in the oven and eaten next day, tasted even better, bringing out the jam flavour.

PEASANT PUDDING

When fruit is plentiful in the country a delicious pudding can be made as follows:

Take a pie-dish and place therein a layer of bread crumbs, then a layer of fresh fruit such as strawberries, raspberries, black or red currants, gooseberries with sufficient sugar to sweeten, another layer of bread crumbs, and so on until the dish is full. Beat up one or two eggs, add as much as is sufficient to moisten the whole and pour over the pudding, allowing the liquid to soak well in, then bake in a moderate oven.

PRINCE ALBERT'S PUDDING

¼lb sugar
¼lb chopped raisins
¼lb flour

3 eggs
Grated rind of lemon

2oz of butter to be beaten till creamy. Add all other ingredients, mixing well, raisins last. To be boiled in buttered pudding dish for 3 hours.

APPLIE PIE

6 ozs. Shortcrust Pastry
1½ lbs. Cooking Apples
2–3 ozs. Demerara Sugar

Peel and core apples; cut and break into chunks; put half the apples in a pie dish; sprinkle with sugar; add the rest of the apples with two tablespoons of water. Cover the pie with rolled-out pastry; decorate with pastry leaf shapes and glaze with milk. Put the pie on a baking sheet in the centre of the oven pre-heated to 400°F. for 35 minutes.

In winter, when there was little variety for fruit pies, mother used figs as a filling. They were soaked overnight, cooked with brown sugar and cut into strips.

KIM'S APPLE PIE

This is a new variation in which the apples are pre-cooked and the pastry rolled very thinly (lining a pie plate and having a crust on top). A scattering of cinnamon, together with a handful of raisins, is added to the apple mixture. Worth making for the spicy scent in the kitchen alone during cooking time, but it tastes particularly delicious, the secret being in the *thin* quality of the pastry, the delicate browning and the succulence of apples redolent with spice.

MINT & CURRANT PASTY

Roll 6 ozs pastry into round. Cover half with 4 ozs currants, sprinkle with sugar and 1 dessert spoon finely chopped mint. Fold over into a pasty, seal edges and prick the top in a few places with a fork. Bake for about 20 minutes at 200°C.

SCROOGE'S REVELATION

PASTRY BASE

12 ozs plain flour
pinch of salt
6 ozs butter
pinch of sugar

Bind together with an egg, after rubbing butter into flour.

SPONGE TOPPING

6 ozs margarine
2 eggs
6 ozs mincemeat
6 ozs sugar
6 ozs self raising flour
2 ozs ground almonds

Line tin with pastry base. Layer with mincemeat. Top with sponge mixture and bake for 40 minutes in a hot oven. Serve warm with double cream. The sponge topping is made like Victoria sponge.

JOSEPHINE'S APPLE CRUMBLE

You need a large, oven-proof dish at the bottom of which place 3 large Bramley apples, peeled, sprinkled with lemon juice, cored and chopped, with generous layers of sugar and a very little water. Set the oven at 190°C and make the crumble:

4oz plain flour
2oz Danish butter
generous sprinkle of cinnamon
2oz soft brown sugar
1oz seedless Californian raisins

Rub the butter into the flour until mixture looks like fine breadcrumbs. Stir in sugar, cinnamon and raisins. Scatter the crumble topping thickly over the apples and bake in centre of oven for $\frac{1}{2}$ hour.

APPLE DUMPLINGS

The apples, as many as required, say 4 or 6 according to number dining, should be washed, peeled, cored and their cavities stuffed with 1oz sultanas, 1oz brown sugar, $\frac{1}{2}$oz butter. This filling, mixed together, is enough for all the apples.

Pastry

8oz S.R. flour
cold water to mix
3oz butter

Make the pastry in the usual way and after rolling out, encase each apple in pastry. Place on baking sheet. Brush dumplings with a little top of milk or egg yolk and bake in a hot oven for $\frac{1}{2}$ hour.

Cakes Scones, Breads and Biscuits

LANCASTER SPICE LOAF

¾ lb Self-Raising Flour
1 teaspoon of Nutmeg
1 teaspoon Cinnamon
1 teaspoon of Ginger
Pinch of Salt
½ lb. Butter
½ lb. Brown Sugar

½ lb Currants
½ lb Sultanas
2 ozs. Chopped Mixed Peel
2 ozs. Chopped Almonds
4 ozs. Glace Cherries
3 Eggs
Milk

Sift flour; add spices and salt; rub in the butter till the mixture is crumbly. Stir in sugar, currants, sultanas, cherries, almonds and peel. Add the beaten eggs and enough milk to give a dropping consistency. Bake for two hours in loaf tins at 350°F.

MOLASSES SCONES

8oz plain flour
1 teaspoon baking powder
8oz wholemeal flour
4oz butter
4oz demarara sugar
1 good handful of raisins

1 teaspoon spice
2 teaspoons chopped candied peel
1 tablespoonful molasses
2 eggs
A little milk

Rub the butter into the flours and baking powder. Add sugar, spice, raisins, peel, molasses. Beat in the two eggs and towards the end, enough milk to make a nice, firm dough.

The Fylde cook broke off small portions, rolled these between her hands, gently flattened the scones, brushed with egg and cooked them on what we now call a metal baking sheet.

These scones are truly "moreish", the molasses giving them an attractive, deep golden colour.

RICH DROP SCONES

4 Cups Self-Raising Flour
2 Tablespoons of Light Golden Syrup
Pinch of Salt
½ Pint of Buttermilk or Milk
3 Heaped Tablespoons of Sugar
2 Eggs

Put flour, syrup, sugar and salt into a warmed bowl; add milk and beaten eggs. Whisk together until mixture is like thick cream. Heat up a greased "griddle" or girdle or heavy frying pan. Drop tablespoons of the mixture at evenly-spaced intervals on the hot griddle. Until you get used to dropping the amount of mixture it is as well to try them singly. When bubbles appear and the bottom is golden brown, turn over and cook the other side of the scone. Serve with butter or whipped cream.

Drop Scones with strawberry jam were served at the Manor, Poulton-le-Fylde, a country mansion which was a favourite wagonette drive for trippers in the early twentieth century from Blackpool and Lytham. Time was allowed to look round the ancient church of St. Chad with its picturesque grounds, replete with trees and leaning gravestones, even then centuries old. People still drive out to see the glorious carpet of snowdrops and crocuses each Spring.

SULTANA SCONES

3oz margarine
1 level teaspoon baking powder
generous handful of sultanas
8oz S.R. flour
2oz caster sugar
a little milk and beaten egg

Rub margarine into flour, add sugar and sultanas. Mix to a soft dough with beaten egg and a little milk if necessary. Knead lightly on a floured baking board and roll out to 1 inch thickness. Cut out scones and place on baking sheet in a hot oven 200°C. In 15 minutes they should be ready, golden brown in colour. The baking powder is best added in the milk.

BUTTERMILK SCONES

3oz butter
8oz flour
½ teaspoon bicarbonate of soda
3oz caster sugar
½ pint buttermilk

Mix dry ingredients together, rubbing in the butter. Dissolve the bicarbonate of soda in the milk. Mix to a soft dough and bake in a hot oven for ½ hour, turning them over in 10 minutes.

ECONOMY DROP SCONES

2oz plain flour
1 dessertspoon caster sugar
1 egg yolk

¼ teaspoon baking powder
5 tablespoons milk
½ teaspoon salt

Sift flour, salt and baking powder into a bowl and stir in the sugar. Make a well in the centre and add the mixed milk and egg yolk, gradually drawing in the flour from the sides by using a wooden spoon until you have a smooth batter. Melt a good nut of butter in the frying pan and drop in teaspoons of the batter. Cook for 3 minutes then turn and brown lightly on the reverse. The scones can be spread with butter, honey, jam or marmalade and can be warmed up next day.

BROWN SODA BREAD

8oz plain flour
3oz porridge oats
1½ tablespoons sugar
1-1½oz fat
½ teaspoon bicarbonate of soda and cream of tartar

3oz wholewheat flour
1 dessertspoon cornflour
½ teaspoon salt
½ pint milk

Rub fat into dry ingredients well blended and mix into a stiffish dough. Shape into 2 cobs and bake on or in greased tins for 25 minutes at 230°C.

WHOLEMEAL DATE AND WALNUT SCONES

3oz margarine
2oz moist brown sugar
1oz chopped dates
milk

4oz wholemeal flour
4oz bran
1oz chopped walnuts

Rub margarine into flour. Add bran, sugar, dates and walnuts. Make into a soft dough with about 1 tablespoonful of milk. Bake in hot oven for about 15 minutes.

WHOLEMEAL DATE SCONES

4oz plain white flour
2 teaspoons baking powder
2oz salted butter
1 egg

4oz wholemeal flour
2oz soft brown sugar
2oz chopped dates
a little milk

Pre-heat oven to 230°C. It is essential to put scones in a hot oven to form a crisp outer coating and spongy interior. Sift baking powder and flour into a bowl. Mix in sugar and rub in butter. Stir in chopped dates, beaten egg and enough milk to make a soft dough. Turn dough onto a floured board and roll it ½ inch thick. Cut out rounds and arrange on a greased baking sheet, brushing tops with milk and egg left over. Bake for 15 minutes. These scones are lovely served warm with or without butter.

WEST YORKSHIRE SCONES

3 cups flour
2 ozs lard
½ teaspoon cream of tartar
½ teaspoon bicarbonate of soda
1 handful of washed, mixed dried fruit

1 cup sugar
2 ozs butter
1 teaspoon baking powder
1 whisked egg and a little milk to mix

Rub fat into flour and dry ingredients. Add sugar and dried fruit. Mix to dough with the beaten egg and milk, using only enough to procure a stiff dough (not wet). Cut out in rounds or triangles, brush tops with what remains of the egg and milk solution and bake for 15 minutes at 200°C.

PUFF PASTRY

8 ozs plain flour
8 ozs cooking fat
pinch of sea salt

cold water and a squeeze of lemon juice

Mix flour and salt in a basin. Cream the fat with a cold knife and rub about 1 oz into the flour. Mix to a soft dough with water and lemon juice. Knead a little until smooth. Roll out the pastry on a floured board. Place the rest of the fat onto the pastry, flattened or cut into small blobs. Fold the pastry over to cover the fat completely and roll round the edges to seal them. Place the fold onto the side. Roll into a longish strip and fold this into three. Roll out again. Repeat this three times, the object being to work the fat in layers throughout the pastry.

Chill in the refrigerator after which the pastry is ready for use. A glazed finish, made with beaten egg brushed onto the surface, enhances the appearance. Oven temperature needs to be high to achieve a light, risen result: 200°C.

FLAP JACKS

8 ozs oats
4 ozs margarine
4 ozs sugar

Cream the margarine and sugar then add the oats. Press firmly into a tin and bake slowly at 150°C. Cut into slices whilst hot. I have also made this flapjack using dark, unrefined Muscovado sugar and a tablespoon of golden syrup, producing a treacly taste, much appreciated in the cold weather.

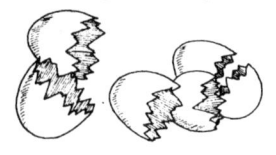

ECCLES CAKES

½ lb short puff pastry
(see recipe)
6 ozs currants
3 ozs sugar
1 oz butter
pinch of spice
few drops of water

Divide the pastry into 8 pieces. Roll into rounds 4-5 ins. across. Divide butter and put into centre of each round with a few drops of water. Wet the edges and put the currants, sugar and spice in the centre and draw up the edges. Flatten with hand, turn over and roll slightly. Prick with a fork and bake in a hot oven for about ½ hour.

LANCASHIRE PARKIN

4oz butter
1 tablespoonful marmalade
3oz moist brown sugar
8oz black treacle
1 egg
¼ pint milk
3oz wholemeal flour
3oz white flour
3oz medium oatmeal
1 teaspoon ground ginger
1 teaspoon mixed spice
1 teaspoon bicarbonate of soda

Place butter, marmalade, treacle and sugar in a saucepan and stir gently over a low heat. When dissolved, add the milk and cool. Pour this melted mixture onto the dry ingredients in a bowl. Add the beaten egg. Pour into a greased, lined cake tin and bake in a very moderate oven for 1¼ hours until firm.

QUICK & EASY PARKIN

1lb flour
½lb syrup or treacle
¼lb lard

2 teaspoonfuls of ginger
1 cup of milk
1 teaspoon bicarbonate of soda

This can be very quickly made in a food mixer, beating all the ingredients together and pouring into a square, well-buttered tin to cook in a moderate oven until firm for about one hour.

LIGHT PARKIN

2 Cups of Wholemeal Flour
¾ Cup of Demerara Sugar
4 ozs. Butter
2 Tablespoons Syrup

1–2 Teaspoons (rounded) Ginger
1 Teaspoon Bicarb. of Soda
Pinch of Salt
1 Egg beaten with a little milk

Place dry ingredients together. Melt butter and syrup over gentle heat; add to mixing bowl. Add sufficient egg and milk mixture to produce a dropping consistency. Bake in a greased tin lined with greaseproof paper in a moderate oven. If stored for a few days before cutting, the flavour improves.

Father's opinion was that a drop of water added to the egg and milk mixture improved the flavour and another of his refinements was to substitute half a cup of fine oatmeal for half a cup of the wholemeal flour. The "ambrosial" touch was produced by finely chopped, crystallised or stem ginger tossed onto the mixture just before it was popped into the oven.

RIBBLE PARKIN

6 ozs plain flour
6 ozs butter
6 ozs medium oatmeal
6 ozs sugar
6 ozs treacle

2 teaspoons ginger
1 large egg
½ pint milk
½ teaspoon baking powder
½ teaspoon cream of tartar

Mix dry ingredients together. Melt butter and treacle together. Warm milk and add to beaten egg. Add butter, treacle, milk and egg to dry ingredients, fold in. Put in greased meat tin and bake for 1 to 1½ hours in a slow oven. Leave in tin to cool. This is better eaten after a few days.

AUNT KATE'S CAKE

4 Teacupfuls of Flour
2 Teacupfuls Sugar
6 ozs. Butter

1 Teaspoon Baking Powder
6 Eggs
A little fresh milk

Mix all the dry ingredients together. Beat the sugar and butter to a cream. Beat the yolks of the eggs and add to the beaten butter and sugar. Now add gradually to this semi-liquid mixture all the dry ingredients, beating all the time.

Next, beat the whites of the eggs to a stiff froth and incorporate with the cake, mixing all well together for ten minutes. Add sufficient milk to make a thick consistency. The excellence of the cake depends on the thoroughness of the mixing and beating. Bake in a moderate oven. Aunt Kate's Cake was decorated with rough almonds cast on before putting in the oven.

LANCASHIRE THRODKIN

1 lb. Coarse Oatmeal
6 ozs. Lard

Good pinch of salt

Rub lard into oatmeal and salt. Mix with a little water. Put into a shallow dish and cook in a slow oven with pieces of bacon cut into strips and placed on top. Eat hot. If any left, it can be broken up, spread with golden syrup and eaten cold instead of cereal for breakfast.

CHOCOLATE VICTORIA SPONGE

4 ozs self raising flour
4 ozs butter
4 ozs fine caster sugar

2 large free-range eggs
2 ozs cocoa or drinking chocolate

Cream fat and sugar until fluffy. Beat in the eggs one at a time, adding a little flour. Fold in flour and cocoa with a metal spoon. It may be necessary to add a little milk for the mixture should never be stiff. Divide mixture into two sandwich tins and bake in centre of oven at 150°C. for ½ hour until well risen and golden. Cool on a wire tray. This makes the basic sponge for the chocolate mousse cake recipe. Rich chocolate cake will be sure to set the taste buds tingling.

GINGER CAKE

8 ozs sieved self raising flour
2 teaspoons ground ginger
pinch of salt
1 tablespoon chopped candied
 lemon peel
8 dried cooking dates cut small

Stir and mix thoroughly in a mixing bowl.

2 ozs brown sugar
8 ozs mixed syrup and treacle
2 ozs butter or margarine
(Weigh on a bed of flour to avoid sticking to the pan)

Melt these in a thick saucepan but do not boil.

Have ready:
¾ teaspoon bicarbonate of soda
 in a warm cup
⅓ cup of milk (gently warmed)
1 egg warmed

Pour the melted contents of the saucepan onto the mixture in the mixing bowl. Stir in like batter, taking a little at a time from the sides. When all has been take up and before it goes cold, break in the warm eggs and beat in as much air as possible. Pour the warm milk onto the bicarbonate of soda (it will froth). Quickly stir this into the batter and turn into greased baking tins. Place instantly into the oven heated at 180°C. and cook for half an hour.

AUNTIE ALICE'S VICTORIA SANDWICH

2 Eggs
4 ozs. Caster Sugar
4 ozs. Butter
4 ozs. Self-Raising Flour

Beat the butter and sugar until light and creamy. Beat in the eggs gradually with some of the flour to prevent a curdled appearance. Gradually stir in the rest of the flour with a metal spoon. Have ready two sandwich tins, warmed, well greased and lined. Divide the mixture equally between them. Place side by side on the first runner of the oven and bake at 350°F. Cool on a wire tray and sandwich the two cakes together with home-made raspberry jam or lemon cheese. Sprinkle liberally with icing sugar.

RICH CHOCOLATE CAKE

3½ ozs dark chocolate
3½ ozs caster sugar
3 ozs sugar syrup
3 ozs grated dark chocolate
   to decorate

4 egg whites
¾ pint whipped fresh cream
1 chocolate Victoria sandwich
(see recipe)

To make a mousse, melt the chocolate in a bowl over a pan of simmering water. Whip the egg whites and caster sugar. Fold in the chocolate and next the whipped cream. Chill in fridge.

    Cut the Victoria sponge cake in two. Moisten the halves with the sugar syrup. Place one half in a 9 ins. cake tin with high sides and a detachable bottom and cover with half of the chocolate mousse. Place the other half of the cake on top of this and again cover with mousse, but leave enough mousse for the sides of the cake. Leave to set and chill for ½ hour, after which the whole cake can be removed from the tin and the sides decorated with the remainder of the mousse and the finely grated dark chocolate.

TRUNNAH CHOCOLATE CAKE

4 ozs. Butter
2 ozs. Cocoa
4 ozs. Flour
2 Eggs

4 ozs. Soft Brown Sugar
Milk
Pinch of Salt
Glace Cherries and Flaked Almonds

Cream the butter and sugar until fluffy. Gradually add the eggs, sifted flour, salt and cocoa with sufficient milk to make a dropping consistency. Place in a well-greased circular tin and bake in a moderate oven for 25 minutes. When cool, cover with melted milk chocolate and decorate immediately with flaked almonds and cherries. Real Morello cherries are a special treat, but don't give your husband too many. Henry VIII liked cherries.

    The Trunnah shops used to put their advertisements in rhyme. J. Clarke of Bridge Terrace wrote:

> "Cakes from Trunnah so delight us,
> That they make our tea sublime,
> And departing make our minds up,
> That we go to Clarke's next time."

The nearby family butcher, James Keirby, on Trunnah Road, Thornton, was famous for his pickled tongues and likewise waxed lyrical about them.

RIBBLE CHEESECAKE

2 ozs butter
4 ozs cheese
   (Cottage or Philadelphia)
4 ozs crushed wholemeal
   biscuits
2 ozs sugar

5 ozs natural yoghurt
small carton whipped cream
1 tablespoon gelatine dissolved
   in 2 tablespoons of water
1 egg yolk

Mix together the butter (melted) and biscuits. Place in a greased, loose-bottomed tin about 10 ins. in diameter. Beat the cottage cheese with the egg yolk, sugar and yoghurt. Fold in the cream and the gelatine. Pour onto the biscuits and allow it to set in the fridge until ready to remove from the tin. The cheesecake can then be decorated with piped cream if desired, although it is rich enough without. Single cherries, raspberries or strawberries are sufficient to set it off, but here lies scope for imagination. On the Christmas tea table it looks festive with cake decorations and holly.

ALMOND CAKE

1 cup butter
½ cup sugar
1 cup finely ground almonds
1 cup plain fine flour
½ teaspoon baking powder

½ cup strawberry jam
4 free-range eggs
   (separate whites from yolks)
1 teaspoon vanilla essence

Cream butter and sugar together. Beat in egg yolks one by one. Stir in vanilla and almonds. Gradually sift into this batter the flour and baking powder. Beat egg whites until stiff and fold in these also. Bake in two sandwich tins for about half an hour until golden brown and firm. When cool, spread the jam thickly between the two cakes. 150°C is the best temperature and this dish is delicious served with whipped cream and a few fresh strawberries.

APPLE SAUCE CAKE

2 tablespoons sugar
½ cup butter

3 cups apple sauce
4 cups fine breadcrumbs

Mix the sugar and crumbs together. Melt butter in a small frying pan and toss the crumbs into it until they brown. Grease a deep-sided baking or souffle dish and spread alternate layers of crumbs and apple sauce inside, starting and finishing with crumbs. Bake for 30 minutes at 190°C.

This "cake", which is more like a pudding, is good with a lemon cornflour sauce, but it can be served cold with whipped cream.

RICH APPLE PIE

4 ozs sugar
3 ozs butter
3 large Bramley apples
1 clove

½ lb pastry
3 egg whites

Gently stew the apples, peeled, cored and cut up, in a small amount of water. Allow to cool slightly then beat in the sugar and butter until the apple is puree. The egg whites should then be whipped until stiff and folded into this puree. Add the clove for flavour. Pour all into a pie dish and cover with a pastry lid. Make a hole in the pastry or insert a pie funnel. Brush the pie lid with a mixture of egg and milk to brown the pastry. Cook for ¾ hour at 200°C.

BURY SIMNEL CAKE

1 lb. Flour
2 ozs. Candied Peel
½ lb. Raw Cane Sugar
1 lb. Currants
½ lb. Sultanas
1 Teaspoon of Mixed Spice
½ Cup of Warm Beer

4 ozs. Chopped Almonds
3 ozs. Butter
2 ozs. Lard
4 Eggs
½ Teaspoon Bicarb. of Soda
1 lb. Almond Paste

Rub fat into flour. Add all the dry ingredients then beat in the eggs and beer, but reserve some of the egg for glazing the almond paste later. Bake in the centre of a moderate oven for about three hours. Cool. Roll out two-thirds of the almond paste to fit the cake, crimping the edges with a fork and fixing it on with runny jam. Make a dozen "eggs" from the remainder of the paste and balance them round the edges, brushing all the paste with the egg reserved. Brown under the grill and decorate with a fluffy, model Easter chicken.

   Traditionally this was prepared four weeks beforehand to be eaten on Simnel or Mothering Sunday, mid-Lent. There was always an annual fierce argument in the kitchen that this version was not real Bury Simnel because the paste was not in the middle of the cake. Mother put the paste on top because if placed in the centre the cake became sad.

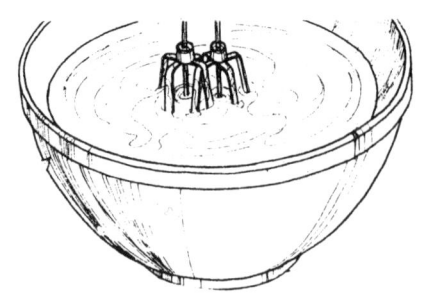

SHORTY CAKE

This is more like shortbread and rich in fats.

6oz caster sugar 6oz butter
6oz lard 10oz plain flour
1 teaspoon baking powder 1 egg

Mix it like shortbread, rubbing fat into flour and adding the other ingredients. Some families roll the mixture into two cakes, spreading apricot jam between, but it is rich enough without. If baked as one round in the cake tin, decorate the top with a forked pattern and scatter well with sugar when baked and cold. It takes 1 hour in a moderate oven.

RICE CAKES

The weight of 4 eggs in flour and ground rice
(two of ground rice and two of flour)
The weight of 4 eggs in loaf sugar
The weight of 3 eggs in butter
The grated peel of one lemon

Whip the eggs for 5 minutes then add the sugar. Add the two flours, which must be well mixed together. Add a little salt. Whip the butter to a cream. Add this just before it is put into a moderate oven. Scatter the grated lemon peel on top.

This receipt makes either Castle Puddings or small cakes baked in patty tins.

GINGER BRAN

9 ozs butter or margarine *3 ozs crushed All Bran*
9 ozs wheatmeal flour *3 level teaspoons ground ginger*
½ teaspoon baking powder *6 ozs soft brown sugar*

Put the flour, All Bran, ginger and baking powder into a bowl. Cut the margarine or butter into pieces. Rub in well with fingertips or use a food mixer, until the mixture looks like breadcrumbs. Add the sugar and mix in well. Put into a greased, shallow tin and press down with a floured fork, working from the edges to the centre. Bake for 30 minutes at 190°C. until golden brown. Cut into squares whilst still warm and leave in the tin. When completely cold the pieces can be taken out and stored in an air-tight tin. The flavour improves with keeping.

POPPY SEED CAKE

8oz bread dough made with wholemeal flour
1oz softened butter
1 teaspoon of poppy seeds
1 beaten egg

Knead the butter and poppy seeds into the dough. Place on a baking sheet. Brush with beaten egg and a scatter of poppy seeds. After it has risen in a warm place for about fifteen minutes bake in a very hot oven for ¾ hour.

CURRANT CAKE

3 breakfast cups of flour
1 egg
1 teaspoon baking powder
1 teaspoonful of sugar
A little ground nutmeg
4oz lard
4oz currants

Rub the lard in the baking powder and flour. Add a little egg to make it into a pastry that rolls out nicely into two equal rounds. Spread currants over one round, sprinkle with the sugar and nutmeg and scatter a little water over all. Cover with the second round of pastry and seal by moistening edges of the rounds and pressing them together with the prongs of a fork. Brush the top with the remaining egg. Prick and bake on sheet in the middle of hot oven.

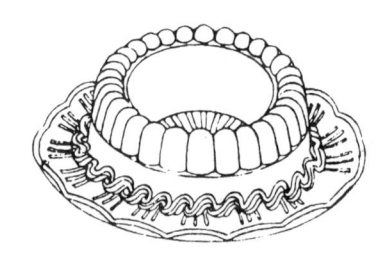

CUT AND COME AGAIN CAKE

1 lb self raising flour
8 ozs butter
8 ozs sugar
3 eggs mixed with ¼ pint milk
½ level teaspoon salt
1 level teaspoon mixed spice
4 ozs currants
4 ozs sultanas

Rub the butter into the dry ingredients. Stir in sugar and fruit. Beat eggs with the ¼ pint of milk. Add to ingredients and mix well with a wooden spoon. Bake in a moderate oven for 1½ to 2 hours or until firm to touch and golden brown.

LANCASHIRE WAKES CAKES

8 ozs plain flour
5 ozs sugar
1 oz currants

4 ozs butter or margarine
1 large free-range egg
milk to mix

Rub fat into flour. Stir in sugar and currants. Mix to a stiff dough with the beaten egg and a little milk. Knead until smooth and roll out the dough ⅛th. inch thick, cutting into rounds. Place on a greased baking sheet and cook in a moderate oven for 15 minutes or until golden brown. Cool on a wire tray, dredging generously with sparkling sugar.

Rolled out thinner and cut into smaller rounds it makes lovely biscuits, but cooking time a little less.

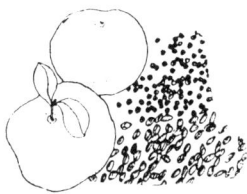

DARK GINGERBREAD

1 lb plain flour
1 tablespoon ground ginger
1 teaspoon baking powder

1 level teaspoon salt
1 level teaspoon bicarbonate of soda

Mix in a bowl:

8 ozs brown sugar
6 ozs black treacle
6 ozs golden syrup

6 ozs butter or margarine
½ pint milk
1 egg

Melt in a pan, then add the beaten egg and milk. Make a well in the mixture in the bowl, pour in the liquid then put in a greased meat tin and bake for about 1¾ hours at 160°C.

DATE AND WALNUT CAKE

8oz flour
1oz margarine
8oz chopped walnuts
8oz chopped dates

1 teaspoon bicarbonate of soda
1 teacup of boiling water
4oz soft brown sugar
1 egg

Put the dates into boiling water. Rub the margarine into the flour and add the sugar, walnuts and beaten egg. Add the date mixture and soda. Bake in a well-greased loaf tin in a moderate oven.

Autumn, with its bonfires of dead leaves and outdoor tidying, calls for . . .

CHORLEY CAKES

1 lb. Rich Shortcrust Pastry *Icing Sugar*
4 ozs. Washed and Dried Currants

Roll the pastry out ¼ inch thick and cut into four rounds about the size of a dinner plate. Place the currants centrally in these circles; moisten the edges and fold together. Press and roll out until the currants show through the pastry. Bake for thirty minutes at 350°F and sprinkle with icing sugar.

    This is very similar to Belthorn Sad Cake which had sugar added with the currants (plus a little water) and was baked in a fire oven. The sugar gently bubbled out and made a brown, shiny topping. A soft, crumbly texture was retained which I find quite impossible to produce in a modern electric or gas oven. Sad Cake just has to have a fire oven to give it perfection.

TOSSET CAKES

1 lb. Plain Flour *1 Teaspoon Caraway Seeds*
1 lb. Butter *1 Teaspoon Coriander Seeds*
¼ lb. Raw Cane Sugar

Crush the seeds with a rolling pin or pestle. Rub the butter into the flour. Add sugar and crushed seeds and leave in a cool place overnight then roll out to ¼ inch thickness. Using a pastry cutter, place the small cakes on a floured baking sheet, sprinkling each with caster sugar. Bake in a cool oven for one hour until firm. The cakes should *not* brown. Dredge thickly with icing sugar when cool and store in an air-tight tin.

    These spicy, sugary cakes were eaten in Stalmine the weekend after August 12th, on Tosset Sunday. The old name of the church was St. Oswald and "Tosset" makes affectionate reference to the saint.

CLUB CAKES

8 ozs. Butter *12 ozs. Plain Flour*
3 ozs. Sugar

The butter and sugar are creamed, the flour worked in either by hand or using a food mixer, and when the dough is rolled out the small cakes can be cut. Baking is in a moderate oven, the finished cakes being liberally sprinkled with icing sugar.

RIBBLE FLAPJACK

8 ozs oats
4 ozs margarine
4 ozs sugar

Cream the margarine and sugar then add the oats. Press firmly into a tin and bake slowly at 150°C. Cut into slices whilst hot. I have also made this flapjack using dark, unrefined Muscovado sugar and a tablespoon of golden syrup, producing a treacly taste, much appreciated in the cold weather.

FAZACKERLEY FLAPJACK

¼lb butter or margarine
1 scant tablespoon golden syrup
sprinkle of sea salt
½lb rolled oats
3oz sugar
1oz dessicated coconut can be substituted for 1oz oats

Melt sugar and butter in a saucepan on low heat. When melted, add oats and nuts if included. Spread mixture, pressing with a fork into a 7 ins by 12 ins swiss roll tin which has been previously well greased. Bake for about 20 minutes in a medium oven. Before it cools, score with a knife into suitable pieces.

ST. HELEN'S SHORTBREAD

12oz butter
1lb plain flour
4oz caster sugar

Cream the butter, gradually adding the sugar. Stir in the flour and knead to a smooth consistency. Press into a porcelain container, prick surface and bake at 150°C for 40 minutes. We found this shortbread delicious and this recipe is also excellent for making crumble toppings on apples, plums, blackcurrants etc. I have used it with fruit conserve which I store for winter use in jars at the bottom of the fridge. However, the timing and the mix are different. Rub in the flour and butter until the "breadcrumbs" stage then add the sugar. Sprinkle thickly on your fruit or conserve and press gently down. Finish off with a final flurry of crumble over the surface and bake in a moderate oven until golden brown. To make a "nutty" shortbread, use half wholemeal, half white flour and muscavado sugar. Press in a topping of 2oz chopped nuts and finish with a sprinkle of white sugar.

CRULLERS

4 tablespoons shortening
2 eggs
1 teaspoon cinnamon
3 teaspoons baking powder

1 cup sugar
3 cups flour
½ teaspoon salt
½ cup of milk

Cream the shortening. Add sugar gradually and beaten eggs. Sift together flour, cinnamon, salt and baking powder. Add one half of this and mix well. Add milk and remainder of dry ingredients to make soft dough. Roll out on floured board to ½ inch thick and cut into strips about 4 inches long and ½ inch wide. Roll in hands and twist each strip, bringing the ends together. Fry in deep fat, strain and roll in powdered sugar. Shortening refers to margarine or lard.

ALMOND CURLS

3oz butter
3oz sifted icing sugar
1 teaspoon rum

2½oz flour
2 egg whites
3oz chopped almonds

Set oven at 200°C. Grease 2 baking sheets. Heat butter very gently till pourable but not oily. Mix together in a bowl the icing sugar, rum, flour, egg whites and almonds. Gently stir the butter into this mixture. Drop in teaspoons on the greased sheets. Bake for 6-8 minutes until browned at the edges. Remove immediately from the baking sheets, shaping them round a rolling pin to make them "curl".

GINGER BISCUITS

1 lb self raising flour
6 ozs sugar
4 ozs margarine
4 ozs lard

8 ozs syrup
1 teaspoon ground ginger
2 teaspoons bicarbonate of soda
    dissolved in 2 tablespoons of milk

Melt the fat in a pan with syrup and add to dry ingredients, adding bicarbonate of soda dissolved in milk last. Mix and knead well. Make into small balls and put onto baking trays. Bake for about 10 minutes at 180°C.

BOURBON BISCUITS

4 ozs plain flour
½ teaspoon baking powder
2 ozs butter

2 ozs castor sugar
1 tablespoon golden syrup
½ oz cocoa powder

FILLING

1 oz plain chocolate
1½ tablespoons water

2 ozs icing sugar

Sieve together flour, baking powder and cocoa. Cream butter and sugar until light and fluffy. Beat in the slightly warmed syrup. Turn the dough onto a board and knead in the flour etc. Roll flat and cut into fingers about 1½ ins. x 2½ ins. Place on a well greased baking sheet. Prick with a fork. Cook for 15 minutes (no more) at 180°C. Cool on a wire tray.

To make the filling, place the chocolate and water in a pan. Heat gently. Beat in icing sugar after removing from heat. Allow to cool, until a spreading consistency is reached and sandwich the biscuits together with this filling. It makes about 15 biscuits.

SPICED COOKIES

1 cup butter
½ cup sugar
2 cups fine self raising flour

1 egg
1 teaspoon cinnamon
1 cup chopped nuts or "nibs"

Cream butter and sugar. Beat in egg. Add flour and cinnamon to mixture. This dough should be chilled for an hour in the fridge, then bits broken off to form balls. On a sheet of grease-proof paper scatter the chopped nuts and roll the balls onto this. Cookies should then be placed on a greased baking sheet for 15 minutes in a hot oven.

CHERRY COOKIES

1 cup softened unsalted butter
½ cup sugar
1 teaspoon lemon juice

3 egg yolks
3 cups self raising flour
small pack of glace cherries chopped

Cream butter and sugar. Beat in egg yolks. Add lemon juice and stir in flour and cherries. Place rough, small portions of the mixture on a baking sheet and bake in a hot oven till set and golden brown, about 15 minutes.

ORMSKIRK BRANDY SNAPS

2 ozs. Plain Flour
3 ozs. Caster Sugar
3 ozs. Golden Syrup
1 teaspoon Brandy
2 ozs. Butter
½ teaspoon Ground Ginger

Grease two baking sheets. Sift the flour and ginger. The butter, sugar and golden syrup should be gently melted in a saucepan. Take off the heat and stir in all the other ingredients. Place teaspoonfuls of this mixture on the baking sheets, allowing room for the mixture to spread. Bake at the top of the oven for ten minutes until golden-brown.* Allow to cool slightly; loosen and roll round the greased handle of a wooden spoon. The brandy snaps will then set in the traditional curled shape. A new way with brandy snaps would be to fill them with whipped cream. *At 350°F.

Sandwich fillings give much scope for the imagination. Different kinds of bread make for variety; some fillings taste specially good with brown bread; fresh watercress is good with coarse wholemeal. Use cheese and sausage, cottage cheese with chives, creamed soft-boiled egg, hard-boiled egg, boiled ham and pineapple, meat loaf, tomato with chutney, sliced capon with sage and onion stuffing, sliced tongue, cold roast lamb, lettuce and tomato. If you use cucumber, cut both bread and cucumber as thinly as possible and use as soon as possible. Slightly dampened paper layered over the sandwiches helps to keep them from drying up in hot weather. Scotch eggs make good filling extras. Thermos flasks are useful for carrying both hot and cold drinks.

OATIES

Since the Romans camped at Ribchester and ate their porridge every morning Oaties, I believe, must have been the natural step forward and have flourished ever since. Easy to make, they are nutty, wholesome and you don't get tired of them. As with all confectionery, oaties taste better made with butter.

10 ozs wholemeal flour
6 ozs butter
4 ozs soft brown sugar
2 eggs
2 tablespoons milk
2 ozs roasted hazelnuts
2 ozs sultanas
4 ozs rolled oats

If you don't use self-raising wholemeal flour add 1 teaspoon of baking powder to give "lift" to the mixture. Cream the butter and sugar. Beat in the eggs and milk. Add the flour, hazelnuts and sultanas. From this stiff dough make about 25 small balls and roll them well into the oats. Place on a greased baking sheet and bake at 180°C, for 25 minutes until golden.

WHITEWELL SHORTBREAD

4 ozs self raising flour   2 ozs caster sugar
2 ozs butter

Rub the butter into the flour until the mixture looks like breadcrumbs. Stir in the sugar and knead until the mixture clings together. Roll out on a floured board, prick with a fork and mark into sections. Bake for an hour at 160°C. This is a thick shortbread (about one inch). 1 oz of cocoa replacing 1 oz of flour will make a chocolate-flavoured shortbread, but the traditional Ribble Valley shortbread is plain, always made with butter and well dredged with a topping of finely ground sugar.

WHEAT BISCUITS

6oz wholemeal flour   1 egg
6oz crushed wheat   Pinch of salt
1 teaspoonful cream of tartar   ½ teaspoonful bicarbonate of
4oz butter   soda
2oz sugar   A little milk

Press the lumps out of the cream of tartar and bicarbonate of soda, and add the salt. Mix them thoroughly with the wholemeal. Add the crushed wheat, rub in the butter and add the sugar. Lastly add the well-beaten egg, together with sufficient milk to mix to a stiff paste. Roll out thinly and put on a greased baking sheet. Bake in a moderate oven at 325F until pale brown and firm.

ROMAN SANDALS

Please do not be put off by the name. This recipe and one other were supplied by an old gentleman with Merseyside connections who has chaffed me for what seems like a century. He believes that an army marches on its stomach and the Romans used lots of oats.

1oz bran   4oz S.R. flour
4oz oats   2oz sugar
4oz margarine   ½ teaspoon bicarbonate of
2 eggs   soda
                                 1½oz currants

Fred says mix up the lot, so do just that (very easy with a food mixer). On the first occasion he got the egg shells in as well and they were pretty gritty, but we have both improved since those days. Roman sandals are very sustaining. Mixed together, you get a nice firm dough. Flour a board. Roll out to about ¾ inch thick and cut shapes. Fred uses a tumbler top to cut a circle. Place on a baking sheet and cook at 190°C for about 25 minutes.

QUICK SHORTBREAD

1lb flour
½lb butter
¼lb sugar

Rub the butter and sugar to a cream. Add the slightly warmed flour gradually. Knead well and press into wheels one inch thick. Bake in a moderate oven till biscuit-brown.

BREAD MAKING

"How wasteful and indeed shameful", wrote William Cobbett in his **Cottage Eeonomy**, "for a labourer's wife to go to the baker's shop. Every woman, high or low, ought to know how to make bread".

He was right. It is easy and its well worthwhile.

The Victorian cook gives no instructions on how to make the dough, but it was probably the basic "recipe":

3lb wholemeal flour
2oz yeast mixed with a little water
1oz lard

1 tablespoon salt
A little brown sugar
1 pint milk

YEAST BREAD

Containing bran or crushed wheat . . .

1¾lb flour
¼lb bran or crushed wheat
1oz lard
1½ teaspoonfuls salt
½oz yeast
Lukewarm water or milk and water to mix

Add the salt to the flour, rub in the lard and add the bran or crushed wheat. Mix the yeast with a little of the lukewarm liquid and pour into the centre of the flour. Add sufficient liquid to mix to an elastic dough. Knead thoroughly and half fill some warm greased loaf tins. Put to rise in a warm place until the dough just reaches the top of the tins. Bake in a hot oven of 450F for ten minutes, then reduce the heat to 400F, and continue to cook until the loaves are brown and sound hollow when tapped. Cool before putting away.

LANCASHIRE LOAF

1 lb plain flour
6 ozs sugar
4 ozs sultanas
4 ozs butter
4 ozs chopped cooking dates

2 tablespoons treacle
2 teaspoons bicarbonate of soda
½ pint milk
½ teaspoon sea salt
2 ozs candied peel cut up

Grease and line two 1 lb loaf tins. Rub the butter into the sieved flour and salt. Add the sugar, sultanas, dates and peel. Beat in the treacle then quickly add the soda to the milk and pour into the mixture immediately. Mix well and divide between the two tins. Bake in the centre of a hot oven at 150°C. for 30 minutes then reduce the heat to 120°C. until cooked, which will take another 15 minutes. This is good sliced and buttered when cold.

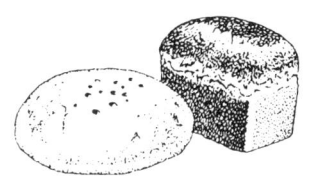

CHRISTMAS BREAD

1 lb flour
6 ozs sugar
4 ozs butter
1 cup sultanas which have been
   saturated in milk
   for half an hour

1 oz yeast
½ pint warmed milk
½ cup almonds
½ cup glace cherries
¼ cup candied peel (chopped)
1 teaspoon grated lemon rind

Cream the yeast with a teaspoonful of sugar and add a little of the warmed milk. Rub the butter into the flour. Add the dry ingredients and the strained sultanas. Mix well with the rest of the warmed milk. Knead, bake in a loaf tin in a hot oven, reducing the temperature after 40 minutes to 120°C.

APPLE & BRAN LOAF

8 ozs wholemeal flour
4 ozs butter
4 ozs brown sugar
2 ozs sultanas
1 oz washed bran

2 teaspoons baking powder
½ teaspoon cinnamon
2 beaten eggs of medium size
2 cooked and pureed apples

Pre-heat oven to 170°C. Grease and line a loaf tin. Mix flour, baking powder, cinnamon and bran together. Cream the butter and sugar and gradually add the beaten eggs. Add half of the flour well sifted, then add the apple pulp and sultanas. Finally add the other half of the flour, mixing well. Bake for about 1½ hours in centre of oven at 170°C.

WHOLEMEAL BREAD

1½ lbs wheatmeal or
   wholemeal flour
1 oz fresh yeast

1 oz lard
2 teaspoons salt
¾ pint warm water

Mix flour and salt. Rub in fat. Blend fresh yeast with warm water and add to flour mixture. Mix to a dough, kneading on a floured board for about ten minutes. Put the dough in a basin placed inside an oiled polythene bag and leave it to double in size, then knead it once more. Grease three loaf tins and divide the mixture amongst these. Bake in a pre-heated oven for 40 minutes at 230°C. The test for whether bread is cooked is made by tapping the base of the loaf. It should feel firm and sound hollow.

HOT CROSS BUNS

It was in the 18th century when hot cross buns became symbols of Good Friday. Liverpool made much of the Easter season, "lifting" being a traditional Easter sport. As far back as the Middle Ages buns came from the bakers wedge-shaped and were known as wigs. Home-made hot cross buns are delicious and worth all the effort of making.

1lb plain flour
3oz caster sugar
4oz warm milk
1 beaten egg

1oz fresh yeast
4oz hot water
4oz salted butter

This is a basic bun mixture to which sultanas etc., can be added and, if hot cross buns are desired, 1 level teaspoon each of cinnamon, ground nutmeg and spice.

    Put flour and spices into a warmed mixing bowl. Crumble the yeast into a basin, add 1 teaspoon sugar and ¼lb flour from the bowl. Make up the warm milk and water to 8oz, using a wooden spoon. Mix this liquid into the yeast, flour and sugar. Leave in a warm place for 20 minutes then mix the rest of the sugar with the flour and rub in the butter. Make a well in the centre and put in the egg and yeast mixture, mixing to a dough. Turn onto a floured board and knead well. Place this dough in a bowl, cover with a warm, clean tea towel and leave to rise for 1 hour. The dough should then be rolled into a sausage shape and cut downwards to form round buns. Brush each with beaten egg, mark with a cross (don't forget) and bake at 230°C until golden brown.

    I am told that the true hot cross bun from this region has its cross made from strips of almond paste and a glazing (2oz sugar and 1 gill of water) boiled up to form a syrup, should be lavishly spread over the cross before baking.

GRANDMA SHORROCK'S MALT LOAF

1lb S.R. flour
4oz dried fruit
1 tablespoon syrup
a little milk

2oz sugar
1 teaspoon baking powder
1 tablespoon treacle

Mix all the dry ingredients then add warmed syrup and treacle together with enough milk to bind. Bake in a moderately hot oven till golden and springy to touch. After two days' storage in air-tight tin serve sliced and buttered.

CRUMPETS

From the 18th century the crumpet and muffin man patrolled Liverpool streets with a handbell and his basket of wares covered with a white starched cloth balanced on his head. He has passed into history but his crumpets are still made.

1lb plain flour
½ teaspoon bicarbonate of soda
½oz fresh yeast

1 pint milk
1 teaspoon salt
5 tablespoons tepid water

First warm flour and have all ingredients warm as in bread making. Warm the milk and use a little of it to cream the yeast. Make a well in centre of flour and pour in milk and yeast mixture. Use an electric beater for about 5 minutes to aerate mixture, which should then be left in a warm place for an hour under a warm, damp cloth. Dissolve bicarbonate of soda in the tepid water when the hour is up, and the dough well risen. Beat this in and leave for a further hour. The crumpets are best baked on a griddle. Turn crumpets to cook on the other side until golden brown. The traditional way with crumpets was to eat them toasted with every hole full of butter, but now they are used with golden syrup, scrambled egg or haddock.

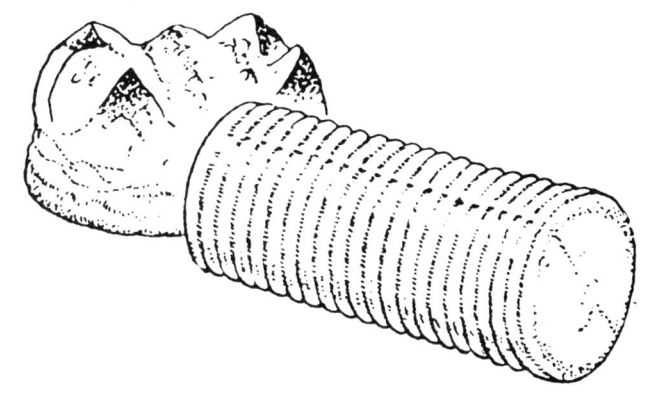

Jams and Sauces

BRAMBLE JELLY

We made this in the days before crop spraying, gathering the wild blackberries in the heart of the country. Nowadays you must be certain that hedges in which the brambles grow (often field boundaries) have not been sprayed, and do not take berries from roadsides where petrol fumes may have coated the fruit with lead.

Gather the berries on a dry day, allowing half a pound of sugar to one pound of fruit and boil for ¾ of an hour. One pound of apples added to three pounds of berries improves the flavour, but where apples are used more sugar must be given (¾ lbs. of sugar to every pound of fruit).

Strained through a jelly bag (before sugar is added) produces a smaller yield for potting, but the resultant clear jelly looks beautiful and tastes fruity. This is also very good for colds in winter time as is blackcurrant jelly dissolved in a little hot water to make a drink.

LEMON CHEESE

¼ lb. Butter
1 lb. Sugar
6 Eggs
Juice of Two Large Lemons

Grate the lemon rind. Have ready a pan of boiling water. Stand in this a stone jar or jug. Put in sieved sugar and butter. When melted, add well-beaten, strained eggs, grated rind and lemon juice. Stir continually until it thickens on back of wooden spoon. When fairly cool, pour into warmed, clean jars.

MARMALADE

Wipe 12 Seville oranges. Cut them up finely, taking away the thick pith and skin in the middle of the fruit. After squeezing the juice and pips into a basin, strain the juice from the pips and pour a pint of boiling water over them, leaving them to soak for 24 hours. Put the fruit when cut up into an earthenware vessel and pour five pints of water onto it. Let this stand for 24 hours. (NOTE. Do not be tempted to omit this process or you do so at the expense of flavour).

Strain the pips and fruit, the liquor from them to be put in a preserving pan with the oranges. Bring to boiling point after adding nine pounds of loaf sugar. Boil fast for a set, about one hour.

PEACH MARMALADE

2 lb. Prepared Peaches
1½ lbs. Sugar
2 tablespoons of Lemon Juice
1 teaspoon Brandy

Pare and stone peaches. Cut up small. Use really ripe fruit. The weight must be calculated after the fruit is prepared. Crack about one quarter of the stones; chop the kernels and cover with cold water. Leave. Place the cutup fruit in a preserving pan and heat slowly, stirring to prevent sticking, as no water is added. The juice will eventually run. Simmer for 45 minutes and add the sugar. Bring to the boil and boil for five minutes. Add two tablespoons of lemon juice and the water from the cracked stones and kernels. Boil for a further ten minutes or until a set is obtained. Pot and cool, covering with a waxed circle dipped in brandy.

BRANDY BUTTER

This recipe is specially recommended to use underneath the lids of hot mince pies.

4oz butter 4oz caster sugar
4 tablespoons brandy

Mix ingredients together as before

MAY'S RUM BUTTER

1lb dark brown sugar
1 glass of rum
¼lb best butter
a little grated nutmeg is optional

Melt butter, then mix sugar, rum and nutmeg. Beat well and let it stand. Don't let the butter go oily. Can be spread on wholemeal bread or sparingly on some cakes.

APRICOT SAUCE

". . . 2 tablespoonfuls of apricot jam
1 teaspoon of butter dissolved in a pan . . ."

Add 1 teaspoon of cornflour. Mix well. Now add the 2 tablespoonfuls of apricot jam with 1 gill of water. Boil well and strain. If too thick, add a little more water.

HARD SAUCE

⅓ cup butter
½ teaspoon flavouring extract
1 cup powdered sugar

Cream the butter until very light. Add sugar very slowly, beating until light and creamy. Add flavouring and beat again. This was poor man's brandy butter.

A SPECIAL VANILLA SAUCE

¼ cup sugar
2 egg yolks
2 cups milk
1 tablespoon cornflour
1 teaspoon vanilla essence

Blend egg yolks, sugar and cornflour thoroughly. Gradually add the milk. Cook for about 5 minutes, stirring all the time. Add vanilla last after removing from heat.

OLD-FASHIONED CHOCOLATE FILLING

3oz unsweetened chocolate
¾ cup powdered sugar
1 tablespoon corn starch
3 tablespoons cream
1 egg
1 teaspoon vanilla extract

Melt chocolate in top of double saucepan, add cream and egg. Mix in sugar gradually. Add corn starch, which has been mixed with a little cold water and cook, stirring constantly until smooth and thick. Add the vanilla. Spread between layers of cake. An old recipe; the corn starch is what we call cornflour.

AUNT ANNIE'S FLUFFY ICING

6oz granulated sugar
3 tablespoonfuls cold water
½ of a level teaspoon baking powder
1 egg white
1 teaspoon orange juice
a little grated orange rind

Put all ingredients except grated rind and baking powder into a basin. Put over a pan of boiling water. Beat mixture with a rotary whisk for 6 minutes. Remove basin and stir in the baking powder. Spread icing over top and sides of your cake and sprinkle with the grated orange rind. Good on a Victoria sponge cake.

Icing can also be made from Philadelphia cream cheese creamed with 4oz of unsalted butter. Add 2 cups of icing sugar and ½ a cup of chopped walnuts. Cream all together and spread onto cake.

NUT HONEY

Juice of 3 Oranges
Grated Rind of 1 Orange
1 oz. Butter

1 oz. Ground Almonds
6 ozs. Sugar
1 Egg Yolk

Cook all together in a double saucepan until the mixture looks like honey. Pot and cover. As a tea-time spread for children this is a winner.

SPICED NUTS

Shell, heat in butter, then toss in a salt spice mixture (cinnamon or ginger). Roasted hazelnuts lend themselves to this.

RUM BUTTER

½ lb. Moist Brown Sugar
¼ lb. Unsalted Butter
2 tablespoons of Rum

½ teaspoon of Nutmeg
¼ teaspoon of Cinnamon

Beat the butter over heat until soft and creamy but do not let it become oily. Mix the spices with the sugar and beat into the butter. Add the rum, beating in each addition. Put into a basin and cover when set. Serve from this basin. In the Lake District, special basins, beautifully decorated and kept in the family for years, were used only for this purpose although brandy, more often than rum, was put in the recipe.

Cold Sweets and Toffee

There is no doubt that Lancashire residents have a sweet tooth and that ginger is a favourite flavour. I was struck by the number of gingerbread and parkin recipes. It was impossible to include all versions of this tots', teens' and grandads' favourite.

Variations sprang from individual cooks' recipes which I did not wish to standardise as long as the method was plain. Preferences deemed to be the best choice, such as free-range eggs, sea salt etc. deserved to remain, but can obviously be adapted. Amongst the tips for sweets, the liberal use of lemon juice emerged: sprinkled on strawberries; in jam making; added to water in which apples are stewed; sprinkled in apple pies; even for improving the taste of mushrooms. To extract all the juice plunge the lemon into very hot water first or warm it in an oven. Two tips from an old source were:
(1) never remove the stalks from strawberries before washing them, and
(2) add a dessert spoonful of strong coffee to improve chocolate mousse.

CHOCOLATE ICE CREAM

½ cup runny honey
1 egg
½ cup grated chocolate

1 cup milk
1½ cups double cream
1 tablespoon cornflour

In a double saucepan heat the milk, adding the honey and cornflour when it has become smoking hot. Stir continually and cook for ten minutes. Beat the egg into a quarter cupful of milk and stir this into the mixture in the double saucepan. Allow it cool before shaking in the grated chocolate and thick cream. Put the mixture into a suitable freezer container. Do not fill to the top. Put into deep freeze and when it appears to be freezing, beat until it has a smooth texture. Replace in the freezer till ready for use.

SYLLABUB

Old English Syllabub was made with milk straight from the cow into wine or cider to make a frothy mixture, sweetened, and flavoured with spices. In Tudor times the cow was milked out in the street or by the hedge. A newer method is to soak the grated rind of one lemon in its own juice for two hours, then add 3 ozs. of caster sugar, two tablespoons of brandy, two tablespoons of sherry. Gently add this mixture to half a pint of whipped double cream until all is blended. Put into goblets and chill before serving.

RHUBARB DREAM

This is best made with apple rhubarb.

1½lb rhubarb
3 dessertspoons gelatine dissolved in ¼ pint of warm water
3 teaspoons lemon juice
8oz sugar

Wash and trim but do not peel the rhubarb, which should be cut into pieces about an inch long and cooked with sugar. Gentle heat and no water gives best results. Strain the gelatine into the pulpy rhubarb. Add the lemon juice and whisk well. Leave to cool then whisk again. Place in individual glasses and serve with cream. A small meringue to decorate gives extra sweetness and "crunch".

CHOCOLATE MOUSSE

2 slabs Menier chocolate (or similar)
burnt chopped nuts
4 eggs
2 tablespoons orange juice

Melt chocolate and orange juice in a bain-marie, stirring until it is like very thick cream. Allow to cool for a bit. Separate eggs; stir yolks into chocolate; whip whites very stiff and fold into chocolate; pour into souffle dish and put in fridge overnight. When set, scatter nuts. A special treat. the recipe is from Meols Hall.

LEMON SYLLABUB

2 tablespoons caster sugar
juice of 1 large lemon and its finely grated rind
½ pint double cream

Whip the ingredients well and turn into individual dishes. This lovely lemon flavour should not be detracted from by adding any decoration.

RASPBERRY FOOL

1 lb raspberries
2 ozs sugar
¾ pint milk
2 large free-range eggs

Beat up the eggs with the sugar and gradually add the milk. Put the custard in a double saucepan and stir till it is thick enough to coat the wooden spoon, but do not allow it to boil. Puree the raspberries in a food blender, or rub through a hair sieve. The custard, when cold, should be strained onto the fresh raspberries and well mixed. Half cream and custard make an even more delicious dish. Strawberry Fool is made in the same way.

WILD STRAWBERRY SYLLABUB

Summer saw Wild Strawberry Syllabub but nowadays the ordinary garden strawberries, or perhaps fresh raspberries, would do.

½ pint thick cream
2 tablespoonfuls of brandy
1 tablespoonful of honey
8oz strawberries

Whip the cream until it forms peaks, then whip in quickly the brandy and honey (don't overdo the whipping).

Gently spoon in the strawberries and put the syllabub into individual cold glasses.

CILLA BLACK FOREST TRIFLE

sponge cake (or any stale cake)
tin pitted cherries
custard powder
double cream
Jordan's apple crunch (alternative)
Rowntree's black cherry jelly
glace cherries for decoration
Cadbury's flake
cherry brandy

Line the base of the trifle bowl with sponge cake (or stale cake) soaked in the juice from the tin of cherries together with a good dash of cherry brandy (or sherry). Make the black cherry jelly, pour on top of sponge cake, mix in the pitted cherries. Allow to set. Make thick custard with custard powder, or for real luxury make an egg custard, pour on top of jelly. When custard has cooled, whisk up the double cream and pipe on top, sprinkle with Cadbury's flake and decorate with glace cherries.

Jordan's apple crunch is also tasty sprinkled on the cream instead. Serve when completely set.

CHOCOLATE CUSTARD

4 large free-range eggs
2 ozs sugar
2 ozs milk chocolate
1 pint milk
½ pint whipped cream
2 tablespoons apricot jam or spread

Beat the eggs well. Grate the chocolate. Heat the milk and sugar which should be poured onto the beaten eggs and strained into an oven-proof dish. Stand this in a baking tin containing warm water. Cover with foil and bake at 170°C. for about 1½ hours. When the custard is firm and cold spread the apricot over the top surface. Pipe or spoon on the cream and scatter the grated chocolate over it. Chill in the refrigerator before serving.

STRAWBERRY MALAKOF

4 ozs unsalted butter
3 ozs caster sugar
3 ozs ground almonds
½ lb strawberries
7½ fluid ozs double cream
½ teaspoon almond essence
18 boudoir biscuits
almond or orange liqueur

Lightly butter a souffle dish. Dip biscuits into almond or orange liqueur and place on end around the dish. Cream butter and sugar, stir in almond essence and ground almonds. Whip cream and fold into mixture. Finally stir in strawberries. Chill in refrigerator. Unmould just before serving and decorate with a few sliced strawberries.

PRUNES WITH FLUMMERY

½ lb prunes, washed and soaked overnight
1 lb cooking apples
juice & rind of 1 lemon
1 pint boiling water
1 oz cornflour
4 ozs sugar
4 macaroons

Pour the water from the prunes into a saucepan with the sugar, lemon juice and thinly cut lemon rind. Boil for 10 minutes. Add the prunes and stew for 10 minutes on low heat. Peel and core the apples, cut into quarters and stew separately with 2 ozs sugar and a cup of water. Mash them when soft. Mix the cornflour with a little cold water and pour onto the apple puree. Stir quickly until it boils then boil for 10 minutes over low heat in order to cook the cornflour. Place the prunes in a glass dish and when cool enough pour the flummery over them. When cold, decorate with the macaroons (see recipe) and whipped cream.

BLACKCURRANT SORBET

½ lb blackcurrants (fresh or frozen)
2 ozs caster sugar
¼ pint sugar syrup (see below)
¼ pint water
1 teaspoon lemon juice
2 egg whites

Cook blackcurrants in the water for 10 minutes. Sieve and set aside the puree to cool. Stir sugar syrup and lemon juice into puree, pour into a freezing tray and freeze until nearly firm. Beat egg whites with half of sugar until stiff then fold in remaining sugar. Break down fruit puree with fork and fold in the egg white, making sure they are incorporated well. Return to freezer and leave until set. It should be a light, snowy texture.

SUGAR SYRUP

2 lbs sugar   1¼ pints water

Heat sugar and water slowly in a thick saucepan until sugar is dissolved. Bring to boil and simmer for 4 minutes. Cool and store in sterilised bottles in fridge.

HONEY SOUFFLE

6 tablespoons clover honey   4 eggs
¼ pint cream

Whip the whites of the eggs until they stand up stiffly in peaks. In another basin, whip the cream well. Place the honey slightly warmed with the egg yolks and heat in a double saucepan until the mixture thickens, but do not let it boil. Cool. Fold the egg whites in very gradually and then the whipped cream. Place in a souffle dish in the fridge until you wish to serve.

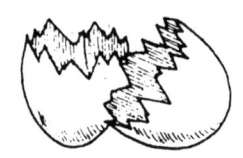

LEMON ICING

Made by stirring two tablespoons of lemon juice into one cup of caster sugar. Beat up to a spreading consistency. Quickly and easily made, the lemon flavour is unbeatable.

FLOATING ISLAND

1 quart milk   4 eggs
4 tablespoons sugar   ½ cup currant jelly
2 teaspoons vanilla or almond
   extract

Scald milk. Beat egg yolks and stir in sugar. Add hot milk gradually, mixing well. Cook slowly in saucepan until mixture begins to thicken, stirring continually. Cool, flavour and put into dish.

Make meringue of whites whipped until dry and into which jelly has been beaten, a teaspoon at a time, and heap on top, or drop meringue by spoonful on top of custard and put small pieces of jelly in centre of each. Chill and serve.

ORRELL HERMITS

Another old recipe

6 tablespoons shortening
1 egg
1½ cups flour
¼ teaspoon salt
1 teaspoon allspice
1 cup chopped, seeded muscatel raisins

1 cup brown sugar
½ cup milk
2 teaspoons baking powder
1 teaspoon cloves
1 teaspoon cinnamon
2 tablespoons chopped citron (candied peel)

Cream shortening, add sugar and beaten egg. Mix well. Add milk very slowly. Sift flour, baking powder, salt and spices together and add slowly. Add fruit, dredged with flour. Drop mixture from a spoon onto greased patty tins and bake in a moderate oven for 15 minutes.

WALNUT AND GRAPE SUNDAE

1½ gills of cream
½ pint milk
4oz sugar
¼ teaspoon gelatine

¼lb grapes
1oz chopped walnuts
Whipped cream
4oz sugar and ½ gill of water for the syrup

Caramelize ½oz of sugar by melting in a saucepan until golden. Soak gelatine in one tablespoonful of milk. Boil the remainder and add the caramel gradually to the milk. Pour onto the gelatine, cool and add cream, sugar, half the walnuts and freeze. Arrange in a mound in the centre of the dish. Decorate with cream and walnuts which remain. The grapes need to be peeled and their pips removed. Cover with cold syrup made by boiling the sugar and water until thick.

What nicer than to return home to currant cake hot from the oven after walking a mile from school?

CARAMEL CUSTARD

Make a custard with two eggs and a pint of milk, a little sugar and four drops of vanilla flavouring. Cook gently and strain. Put 2oz of castor sugar and the juice of a lemon into a buttered mould. Place the mould on the stove and let the sugar cook until a deep golden colour which is caramel, then turn the mould round so that the inside is entirely lined with caramel. As soon as the mould is lined dip it at once into cold water to set the caramel, then pour the custard straight into the mould. Stand in a tin of water and bake in a moderate oven until the custard sets, then turn out.

WINTER FRUIT SALAD

2 tablespoons caster sugar
1 miniature bottle Grand Marnier
1 pineapple
1 lemon
½ melon

2 Cox's orange pippins
2 oranges
2 bananas
6 glace cherries

Peel and chop pineapple, removing fibrous centre. Mix with chopped cherries and cover these with the sugar and liqueur. Leave to stand for 3 hours. Peel quarter and chop the apples. Peel and cut up oranges, removing all pith. Cut melon into cubes, removing outer skin and pips. Peel and slice bananas into rounds. Mix all together including the marinaded pineapple and cherries. A syrup, made by boiling 2oz sugar and a wineglass of water with a lemon cut into slices, can then be poured over the fruit salad. Allow to cool and serve with ice cream or whipped cream.

BUTTER TAFFY

3 cups brown sugar
¼ cup water
4 tablespoons butter

½ cup molasses
¼ cup vinegar
1 teaspoon vanilla essence

Boil sugar, molasses, water and vinegar. When a drop crisps in cold water, add butter and cook for 3 minutes. Add vanilla and cool on buttered pans and break into pieces.

PEANUT BRITTLE

2 cups chopped roasted nuts   3 cups granulated sugar

Put sugar in frying pan and stir slowly over fire. It will lump, then gradually melt. When a pale coffee colour and clear, add nuts and pour quickly on a greased tin. Crack into pieces when cold.

WALNUT TOFFEE

1 lb granulated sugar
3 ozs butter
3 ozs shelled walnuts
¾ gill water
½ teaspoon cream of tartar

Grease a toffee tin and arrange the walnuts in rows. Melt butter in the water, add sugar and bring to the boil. Put in the cream of tartar and boil till a small drop of the toffee, placed in cold water, sets hard. Pour into tin. You need a small toffee hammer to crack up into small portions when cold. This recipe from Bolton-by-Bowland was written down in 1942 when butter was rationed.

CREAM TOFFEE TO CHEW

Melt 1lb of crushed sugar into ¼lb of butter. When nearly melted, add by degrees ½ pint of cream, stirring all the time. Boil until it is so thick you can hardly turn the spoon. Turn it into a tin which has been buttered. Smooth with a clean knife. In a few minutes it will be ready to cut into squares. A quarter of an hour is usually long enough to boil, and be careful for it easily burns. Stir without ceasing, adding a ¼ teaspoon of vanilla just before finish.

EVERTON TOFFY

This 90 years-old "receipt" for Everton Toffy is taken as written in the old recipe book used by "Aunt Kate".

"Take three pounds of best brown sugar and boil with one and a half pints of water until the candy hardens in cold water. Then add one half pound of sweet-flavoured, fresh butter which will soften the candy. Boil a few minutes until it again hardens and pour into buttered trays. Flavour with lemon if you desire."

COTTAGE CANDY

1 lb. Soft Brown Sugar
¼ lb. Butter
4 tablespoons Milk

Melt ingredients over low light then boil gently until mixture thickens. Remove from heat and beat hard until creamy. Pour into buttered tray and mark into squares while still warm.

DAD'S TREACLE TOFFEE

1 lb. Demerara Sugar *Small tub of Cream*
½ lb. Treacle *2 tablespoons of Water*
¾ lb. Butter *Pinch of Cream of Tartar*

Put the water into a pan; add sugar and treacle and a small amount of the butter. Heat very slowly so as not to burn the mixture. Thinly slice the rest of the butter and add gradually with the cream of tartar. Bring to the boil. Test a small quantity by dropping into cold water. If it forms into a hard lump it is ready. Allow to cool down but not set. Stir in the cream and pour into a flat toffee tin or the kind in which you make Swiss Roll. It very quickly sets. You need a small toffee hammer to break it into mouth-sized pieces which can then be wrapped in screws of greaseproof paper.

    This was always a great stand-by in foggy weather. Marching to school with a thick, one-foot-wide, woollen scarf tied cross-wise over your chest and secured at the back with a huge safety pin, you popped a piece of this toffee into your mouth to "keep out the cold" just as you stepped into the street. The day I tried to twirl the milk kit in a swift circle, attempting to defy the law of gravity but managing only to flood the passage floor (I had resisted the temptation for weeks) I didn't get any treacle toffee.

Drinks

Home brewing has flourished for centuries in the Ribble Valley. Pubs with names to conjure with like Bay Horse, Fielden's Arms, The Pippin, Royal Oak, Black Bull, Windmill, Pack Horse, Ribblesdale Arms, De Tablay Arms, Shireburn Arms, White Bull, once had their own brew houses. Buckets of dandelions and spring green nettles can still be gathered weaving towards Ribchester along enticing country lanes that swoop up and down like the Big Dipper: Goose Foot Lane; Gib Lane; Jenny Lane; Gallons Lane; Nab's Head Lane; Allum Scar Lane, Green Lane, names full of history. Coffee made from freshly ground beans tasted great in Clitheroe on a cold January day when snowdrops were blooming on the river banks; home-made Lemonade was a favourite in Longridge by midsummer.

BROOM WINE

The scent of broom in May sunshine made us think of wine-making.

4 pints broom flowers
8 ozs chopped raisins
thinly pared rinds of 4 lemons and their juice
1 gallon of boiling water
4 lbs sugar preferably light brown
½ pint cold tea
2 ozs yeast

Pour boiling water over the broom flowers and leave them for four days, stirring occasionally. Place the fruit juice, peel, tea, sugar and raisins in another container and strain the liquid upon them. Add the yeast, sprinkled on top, and leave the wine in a warm place for nine days. Strain it into a gallon jar and rack off and bottle as the wine clears. Keep until Christmas.

DANDELION ALE

8 ozs fresh, well washed dandelion leaves
1 tablespoon dried yeast
4 teaspoons brown sugar
1 gallon water
1 lemon
1 oz cream of tartar

Thinly pare the rind off the lemon and put it in a preserving pan with the water and dandelion leaves. Bring to boil and boil for at least ten minutes. Put the sugar and cream of tartar into a container into which the strained liquid should be poured. Stir and cool. Add the lemon juice and sprinkle the dried yeast on top. Cover well and leave in a warm place to assist fermentation. After four days, rack off and bottle the beer, adding sugar at the rate of one teaspoon to the pint. It takes about ten days for the beer, left undisturbed, to become clear, when it is ready to drink.

NETTLE BEER

1½ lbs young, well-washed nettles
1 lb demerara sugar
1 tablespoon dried yeast
½ oz ginger

2 lemons
1 oz cream of tartar
1 gallon of water

Boil the nettle tops with the ginger, lemon rinds and water. Simmer for ¾ hour. Strain this liquid onto the lemon juice, cream of tartar and sugar. Stir and cool. Sprinkle the yeast on top. The method thereon is the same as for Dandelion Beer, although waiting time is a week for the tightly sealed bottles to clear.

DANDELION AND GINGER WINE

End of April and into May is the time to make this Ribblesdale brew. All the way from Samlesbury to Ribchester multitudes of golden glowing dandelions smiled down the winding lanes and across the fields.

1 gallon dandelion heads
1 gallon boiling water
8 ozs raisins
5 lbs sugar
½ pint of cold tea

1 lemon
1 oz ground ginger
1 orange
yeast

The flowers should be covered with the boiling water, left for three days and stirred frequently. The liquid should then be strained and the ginger, orange and lemon rinds added. Bring to the boil and simmer for 35 minutes. Now squeeze the juices from the lemon and orange and add immediately to the raisins and sugar in another container. Upon this should be strained the cool liquid. Add the tea and sprinkle about 2 ozs yeast on top. Cover and leave in a warm place to ferment for 8 days. Strain the wine into a one gallon jar. As the wine clears it can be bottled. Keep till Christmas.

MEAD

Use heather honey for preference, the real English variety. Soft water areas produce the best mead so Lancashire may have the edge over Yorkshire here. Almost certainly, mead of this type would be produced by the monks of Whalley and Sawley Abbeys centuries ago.

1 gallon water
1 large lemon
2 ozs yeast
2 egg whites
2½ lbs heather or clover honey

Dissolve the honey in the water, stirring until dissolved. Beat the egg whites and stir them into the mixture. Still stirring all the time, simmer this, skimming away any scum. Cool. Mix the yeast with a little sugar and water and add to the mixture. The peel and the juice of the large lemon is added last. Allow to ferment slowly in a jar with an airlock. Siphon into sterilised bottles, filtering as you go. Store until required. The monks kept it 4-6 years.

HOT TODDY

2 tablespoons rum
¼ pint hot water
2 slices lemon
1 tablespoon caster sugar
juice of 1 lemon

Mix rum, sugar and lemon juice. Pour on hot water. Pour into glasses and top with a slice of lemon.

SNOWBALL

6fl oz advocaat
2 teaspoons cherry brandy
1 pint lemonade
maraschino cherries

This is sufficient for two. Divide the advocaat between two glasses. Almost fill each with lemonade. Add 1 teaspoon cherry brandy to each glass and whisk well. Serve with maraschino cherries on cocktail sticks skewering thin twists of orange.

ADVOCAAT

1 bottle light sherry
1 tin Nestles milk
4 eggs
1 dessertspoon brandy

Mix all these together very well and put in bottles.

BLACKCURRANT PUNCH

¼ pint blackcurrant cordial
rind and juice of 1 orange
½ teaspoon powdered nutmeg
1 pint water
juice of ½ lemon
2 tablespoons brown sugar

Use a stainless steel saucepan into which you place cordial, water, thinly peeled rind of orange, sugar, nutmeg and lemon and orange juices. Bring this slowly to boil after which it should be allowed to stand for ½ hour. Strain and reheat before serving to guests on party arrivals.

MEAD OR HONEY BEER

5 lbs. Honey
¼ oz. each of Bay Leaves, Thyme, Rosemary
1 oz. each of Mace, Nutmeg and Sliced Ginger
½ Teacupful of Malt
2 ozs. Yeast
3 Gallons of Water

Boil the honey in two gallons of water for ¾ of an hour. Take the bay leaves, thyme, rosemary and boil for ¾ of an hour in the other gallon of water. Put this into a tub or earthenware crock with the malt. Stir frequently and when it is lukewarm, strain it. Pour it back into the tub and add the honey and water. Spread the yeast on pieces of toast and lay it on the surface. When the surface is covered with yeast, skim it off. Put the mixture in a barrel. Bruise the mace, nutmeg and sliced ginger; tie them in a piece of muslin and suspend them in the mixture by a piece of string. The mead will take about 48 hours to settle. It is then ready for use.

GRANDAD'S HERB BEER

In two gallons of water boil a few handfuls of the fresh young plants of stinging nettle, a few handfuls of dandelions and 2 ozs. of bruised ginger. (Nowadays it goes without saying that you must be particular about where you gather your nettles and dandelions and they must be thoroughly cleansed.) Boil all together for half an hour and strain. Place into it some pieces of toasted bread on which has been spread a small quantity of brewer's fresh yeast. When the process of fermentation is over add 1 oz. cream of tartar. (Grandad kept his "brew" by the fire oven to help the process.) Strain, bottle and cork the beer. He always used screw-top stone jars for this; never glass bottles. The were then laid on their sides in a cool place and the herb beer was ready for use within a few days. When I was about four I saw him open a jar. The screw top took off like a genic and herb beer spattered the ceiling. I was very impressed.

ELDERBERRY WINE

8 lbs. Ripe, Black Elderberries
1 gallon Water
3 lbs. Demerara Sugar
½ teaspoon Whole Allspice

1 oz. Ground Ginger
1 teaspoon Cloves
1 oz. Yeast
Slice of Toast

Strip the elderberries from their stalks. Pour the water over them. Mash the fruit well and leave for five days to extract all the juice, stirring well every day. Strain juice into preserving pan with sugar, allspice, ginger and cloves and boil for half an hour. Allow to cool and strain. Spread the yeast on a piece of toast; float it on top of the liquid; cover and leave to ferment for a week, stirring daily. Skim; strain off into a cask and leave the bung loose until fermentation has ceased. Then hammer the bung in tightly; leave for four months and then bottle.

RASPBERRY VINEGAR

Cover a large dish of raspberries with sugar and allow to stand for 24 hours or more till you can drain one pint of juice. Set aside. Stir into the strained fruit one pint of vinegar; strain again and add the liquid to the juice you set aside. Add two pounds of sugar. Simmer gently until syrupy. Allow to cool. Bottle when cold. The syrup may be used on pancakes instead of lemon, taken in hot water as a remedy for a cold, or put on plain vanilla ice cream.

ORANGEADE

4 Oranges
6 ozs. Sugar
1½ pints Water

Wash and dry the oranges. Thinly remove the zest from one orange. Put zest and sugar in a jug. Boil with ½ pint of the water. Stir until the sugar has dissolved. Cover and allow to infuse. Add the remaining cold water and the juice squeezed from the oranges. Don't leave the juice standing for long as it loses in vitamin C content. Strain into a glass jug.

COFFEE LIQUEUR

Grind 3 ozs. of best, freshly roasted coffee. Prepare a syrup with 1 lb. of sugar and half a pint of water. Put the coffee into the boiling syrup and boil for a few seconds. Mix all with one quart of brandy. Cork well and let it stand for one month. Filter and the liqueur is ready for use.

APRICOT DRINK

A new recipe, using 4 oz. dried apricots, 1 pint of milk, 2 tablespoons of Grand Marnier.

Cover washed apricots with milk and leave to soak overnight in a cold place. Pour into goblet of electric mixer. Blend and strain. Add the Grand Marnier, slowly stirring in well.

DAMSON GIN

This old recipe requires:

3 lbs. Damsons
3 lbs. Sugar
1 Large Bottle of Gin

Place well washed damsons in a large jar with a screw top. Put sugar over the top and pour the gin over. Screw down and keep until Christmas, then pour off the liquid and bottle.

RASPBERRY WINE

3lb raspberries   *1oz yeast*
6 pints water   *1½lb sugar*

Boil the sugar and water to make a syrup and pour it over the mashed raspberries. When cold, add the yeast and leave for two days. Strain and bottle, adding a little more sugar.

Old Remedies

LAVENDER POT POURRI

Mix well together dried and free of stalk:
½lb lavender flowers   ½lb thyme
½oz mint
Add 1oz dried common salt, ¼oz ground cloves, ¼oz ground caraway. Keep in a crock or jar.

POT POURRI 1820 RECIPE

Pick your roses at mid-day when the dew has gone from them and remove the stems. Spread to dry on sheets of white paper, but not in the sun. When they are dry, mix them with any other dry, scented flowers: pinks, violets, orange blossom, lemon verbena or dried lavender. Add 1oz each of cloves, mace, cinnamon, all spice, thin slices of lemon peel and rosemary. Mix well.

WEST DERBY COUGH MIXTURE

4fl oz olive oil   2fl oz raspberry vinegar
¼lb honey   1 piece of camphor (size of a pea)

Place olive oil and camphor in a jar in the oven until hot. Allow to cool and then add honey and vinegar.
Dose: 1 teaspoon night and morning. Shake bottle well before use.

SKIN LOTION

Mixture of half and half rose water and witch hazel. Mildly astringent. Keep in fridge.

FENNEL WATER

A tonic and antiseptic lotion for the skin. "Sling a handful of fennel in a pint and a half of water and bring to the boil. Simmer for 15 minutes then cool and store in a clean bottle. This must be used in 10 days unless kept in fridge."

OTHER LOCAL PUBLICATIONS

The History of Lancashire Cookery

Tom Bridge takes us deep into Lancashire's culinary past to reveal the classic dishes of the region.

ISBN 1 872226 25 6 £4.95

Includes a facsimile reprint of the U.C.P. Tripe Recipe Book from 1934.

The Lancashire Witches

(W. Harrison Ainsworth)

A beautiful illustrated edition of the most famous romance of the supernatural.

ISBN 1 872226 55 8 £4.95

Completely Lanky

(Dave Dutton)

Combining two best sellers - Lanky Panky and Lanky Spoken Here with additional copy.

ISBN 1 872226 61 2 £4.95